Social Skills For Kids

Over 75 Fun Games & Activities for Building
Better Relationships, Problem-Solving
& Improving Communication

Janine Halloran, MA, LMHC

Published by
PESI Publishing & Media
PESI, Inc
3839 White Ave
Eau Claire, WI 54703

Cover: Amy Rubenzer
Editing: Jeanie Stanek
Layout: Jennifer Wilson-Gaetz & Amy Rubenzer

ISBN: 9781683731450

Printed in the United States of America.

PESI
Publishing
& Media
www.publishing.pesi.com

About The Author

Janine Halloran is a Licensed Mental Health

Counselor who has been working with children, adolescents, and their families for over 15 years. She has a wide range of experiences, including working in schools as an Adjustment Counselor and running social groups in private settings. She is the Founder of Encourage Play, a site dedicated to helping kids learn social skills through play.

Janine is an *NBC Toolkit Parenting Expert* on the topic of Social & Emotional Skills. Janine has also written for Confident Parents, Confident Kids, Hey Sigmund and Bay State Parent Magazine. She has been a guest on the We Turned Out Okay podcast, the Lose the Cape podcast and has been interviewed by the Boston Globe.

She is also the Founder of Coping Skills for Kids and the author of the *Coping Skills for Kids Workbook*, written for elementary school aged kids to help them learn to cope with stress, anxiety, and anger. Janine lives in Massachusetts with her husband, son, and daughter.

Dedication

This book is dedicated to my sister, Johanna.
She was my first playmate and is my
lifelong friend and encourager. Thanks
for playing Monopoly, setting up grocery
stores with me, and creating the most
fun whenever and wherever we played.
And thanks for continuing to encourage
me to make more time for play now!

Table of Contents

Working Together

Taking Turns

Communication

Personal Space

Being Kind

Feelings Identification

Coping with Feelings

Self-Regulation

Respect Yourself and Others

Taking Someone Else's Perspective

Picking Up on Clues

Introduction

Creating Teachable Moments to Teach Social Skills

How many times has this happened to you? You're talking with one of your students - let's call her Justine. You've been working with Justine on some social skills, especially taking turns during games at recess. You talk with her about what it means to take turns, why it's important and you may even do a worksheet on how to take turns. Maybe you role play with Justine about what she can do the next time she wants to play her favorite recess game, foursquare. You feel like you've made some progress, and she's really getting it. You send her out to recess, feeling hopeful. Five minutes later, Justine and another little girl show up in your doorway, crying. The lunch monitor comes up behind them and explains that Justine came over to the foursquare game, jumped into the game without waiting for her turn and accidentally knocked the other student down. You say "We just talked about this. What happened?"

When we see kids who struggle with social skills, it's hard to watch. We want to support them and teach them socially acceptable ways of interacting. So, we talk to them, maybe we do worksheets and talk about what's expected. And they can tell us exactly what the expectations are in those social situations. But somehow that knowledge doesn't translate into real life experiences. How do we teach social skills so that kids will act in expected ways? How do we teach them and have them translate those skills into other areas in their life?

I believe we should start teaching social skills by playing.

Play is the most natural way children interact with the world and learn about it. Dr. Stuart Brown has done extensive research on play both in the animal world and in the human world. In his book, *Play: How It Shapes the Brain, Opens the Imagination, and Invigorates the Soul*, he states that play "isn't the enemy of learning, it's learning's partner. Play is like fertilizer for brain growth. It's crazy not to use it" (Brown, 2010).

Dr. Brown also explains that "learning and memory also seem to be fixed more strongly and last longer when learned in play" (Brown, 2010). It makes sense we should be using play to teach kids social skills.

Children can learn about problem-solving, advocating for themselves, making decisions, working in groups, sharing, and resolving conflicts all by playing. As children develop and grow, so does their way of playing. Mildred Parten (1932) did some great work observing youngsters at play and formulated the stages of social play for children. Let's take a brief look at precisely how social play develops and changes over time for children. There are six stages of social play, and it starts at birth.

1. **Unoccupied Play**

   I know this can be hard to believe, but play starts at birth. You know those random movements that infants make with no clear purpose? This is the beginning of play.

2. **Solitary Play**

   This stage, which starts in infancy and is common in toddlers, is when children start to play on their own. When engaged in solitary play, children do not seem to notice other children sitting or playing nearby. Just because it starts in infancy and toddlerhood doesn't mean it needs to stop. All age groups can (and should!) have some time for independent, solitary play.

3. **Onlooker Play**

   Onlooker play happens most frequently during the toddler years but can happen at any age. This stage is when children watch others play. The child who is looking at the others who are playing may ask questions of other children, but there is no effort to join the play. This may happen when a child is shy, or unsure of the rules, or is hesitant to enter the game.

4. **Parallel Play**

   Parallel play is usually found with toddlers, although it happens in any age group. Parallel play starts when children begin to play side-by-side with other children without any interaction. Even though it seems like they are not interacting, they are paying attention to each other. This is the beginning of the desire to be with other children. This stage starts to lay the groundwork for the more complex social stages of play.

5. **Associative Play**

   At around three to four years of age, children eventually become more interested in the other children rather than the toys. At some point, a child will start interacting more with the other child they are playing with; this is called associative play. They start asking questions and talking about the toys and what they are making. This is the beginning of understanding how to get along with others. During associative play, children within the group have similar goals (for example: building a tower out of blocks). However, they don't set rules, and there's no formal organization.

6. Social Play

Children will begin to socialize starting around three or four. They begin to share ideas and toys and follow established rules and guidelines. They play shop and figure out who will play what role. They can work together to build something or maybe play a simple game together. This is really where a child learns and practices social skills, like cooperating, being flexible, taking turns, and solving problems.

As children proceed through the stages of play, their play becomes more complex and involves more and more interacting with others. For children to practice social skills like cooperating, compromising and problem-solving, the best way to do that is to let them play. They'll remember the rhythms and melodies of social interactions much more smoothly if we allow them the time and space to play.

Social skills are complex and can encompass so many different types and layers of skills. But learning social skills is a vital component of the social and emotional development of children. The Collaborative for Academic, Social, and Emotional Learning (CASEL) is the "nation's leading organization advancing the development of academic, social and emotional competence for all students" (About CASEL, 2018). They have a wealth of information about Social Emotional Learning and have identified five main areas of social and emotional competence. These are self-awareness, self-management, social awareness, relationship skills, and responsible decision-making. Using the CASEL framework (CORE SEL Competencies, 2017), here's what we might expect to see from elementary school students who are developing their social skills:

Self-Awareness

- Recognize and accurately label simple emotions, getting more in-depth as they get older

- Start to identify personal competence ("I'm good at math") which isn't always accurate at a younger age. As they get older, they get more precise about what they can and can't do

Self-Management

- Can describe steps of setting and working toward a basic goal

- Regulate and control impulses in most situations. As they get older, they become more balanced in coping with frustration or failure

- Can use calming strategies

- As they get older, can demonstrate conflict resolution skills with peers, including talking through issues

Social Awareness

- Can identify cues to indicate how others feel and the consequences of those feelings

- Will notice how their own behavior affects others, and with time may modify behavior as a result of realizing the impact their behavior has on others

- Show more complex emotions over time

- As they get older, demonstrate knowledge of social customs for when and to whom certain emotions are appropriate to express

- Over time, they start to acknowledge other people's perspectives

Relationship Skills

- Develop close friendships that are mutual, based on time spent together, shared attributes and overlapping interests. As they get older, they have a more fleshed out understanding of friendship - able to look at qualities in a friend, can start to evaluate friendships

- Playing together can include imaginative, dramatic play and games with rules (board games, sports games)

- Communicate needs, wants, and emotions in healthy ways

- As they mature, they can participate in games with more abstract rules and can make up elaborate fantasy games and situations

Responsible Decision-Making

- Identify a range of decisions they make throughout their lives (what to eat for lunch, what games to play at recess, what to participate in after school, etc). As they mature, they can identify a more complex range of decisions they make throughout their lives

- Can discuss pros and cons of a choice

- As they age, they can have conversations about more complex choices and see nuances

So now we know, play is the best way to learn. We also know that children can develop social and emotional skills, just as they develop other skills in their life.

But what about those kids who are struggling to make it through? The kids we see who are lagging behind in developing their social skills? Like Justine from the beginning of the introduction?

Rick Lavoie, the author of *It's So Much Work to be Your Friend* (2006), writes about those kids who struggle in the social sphere. He talks about the spiral of social skills to help kids who struggle develop these important parts of themselves. First, you learn the skills, then apply and use them in real social situations. Those positive interactions make it more likely that your circle of friends will grow, allowing for more social opportunities, and chances to practice those skills. To get better at the skill, you need to use it in real situations.

For those of us running groups, I'd like you to think of your time with kids in group as one of those real-life situations. If kids are coming to us to be in a social skills group, it means they have struggled in this area, and probably haven't had much success in other social arenas. We want to do the best we can to teach them the skills, AND give them those real-life opportunities to practice.

We know how to talk to kids about social skills. We can have the conversations. Now it's time to create the experiences for them so that they can practice what it feels like to use these social skills in real places. Because they are in a group, we adults can act as scaffolds for them - helping gently guide them to more prosocial behavior in groups and complimenting and reinforcing their positive interactions. Let's create these real-life teachable moments to help support children as they continue to grow and develop in their social repertoire.

How to Use This Book

If you run any social skills group, no matter if you are a school counselor, social group leader, occupational therapist, speech therapist, licensed mental health counselor, psychologist, etc., this book is for you. If you want to get out of the routine of using worksheets, role plays or more traditional group activities; this playful approach is a good alternative. You can pick up the book and find a topic that your particular group needs to work on, read the lesson and set it up pretty quickly. We are all busy professionals, and this book makes it easier for you to create meaningful and practical social skills group experiences.

Each chapter focuses on one particular social skill. At the beginning of each chapter, there's a brief introduction to each social skill topic and some key discussion points you can use to guide the conversation in the group before the activity. Then there are five different activities related to the topic, complete with directions and printables when needed. I've also included some ideas for variations and modifications for the games and activities.

There are a few different types of playful lessons for groups included in the book:

Games & Activities

Just playing different games and doing playful activities is a perfect way to learn skills. By setting up group play situations, kids will work on at least a few social skills at the same time. Teachable moments will occur, and kids will naturally practice social skills.

Group Challenges

Giving kids group challenges also works wonders for creating these teachable moments. Often, the kids love the idea of a group working together to accomplish something or to reach a goal. It can give them confidence when they make it through. It's also an opportunity for them to have a shared positive experience with their group members.

Visual Lessons

Using visuals is a powerful way to teach kids. Often those are the lessons that stick longer because incorporating a visual is such a useful learning tool. I've also included some visual lessons to target a few different social skills.

Creative Outlets

Kids benefit from being creative. They work on being flexible and thinking about things differently, especially when they see the variety of ways other kids create with the same prompt. Some lessons have kids create their own item to take home to use or reference later.

Learning social skills happens over time, and you often need to circle back to the same skills to have kids understand and solidify the teaching. That's why, in addition to the listed activities, at the end of the book I also list a few more ideas to extend the learning on each particular skill. I suggest other books, games, products, videos or other activities for additional learning opportunities around that specific skill. These suggestions can help you as a group leader to create more lesson ideas for a particular topic or if you want to use different types of media in your work.

While the activities in the book are listed under one particular social skill, they can be used for others as well. Often, one game or activity encompasses a multitude of social skills. In real life, you use more than one social skill at a time. For example, when you're working together you also have to work on your listening skills, compromising and using a kind tone. Although this book is written to focus on one social skill at a time, a lot of the activities in this book can be used for developing a variety of social skills - you as the group leader decide which social skill should be the focus for that group lesson.

Please remember that the group plan doesn't have to go perfectly. Most likely, it won't. Instead of thinking of it as not going perfectly, reframe it as a teachable moment. It's about your intention. The experience is all you need.

In general, smaller groups or groups with a low student-teacher ratio work well, because if multiple teachable moments are happening at the same time, you want to be able to intervene adequately and address the students' needs. This is also a great opportunity to involve interns, so they can support kids in the group and learn ways to set up and work through teachable moments with children.

How to Debrief After an Activity

After each game/activity, there are some follow-up questions to ask the group to help solidify the learning. These questions can help group members get a deeper understanding of each skill and how the activity they did or game they played connected to that particular skill. The questions listed are just a jumping off point. Use what you saw during the group and ask about it. For example:

"Dina, I noticed that you were getting frustrated and Tom helped you. What did that feel like for you, Dina? And what about you Tom?"

You can always start off the debriefing activity with a simple query – what was your favorite part of this activity? What was your least favorite part?

Also, use your group dynamics knowledge as you lead the lessons and discussions. Establish the group with a set of rules that everyone in the group agrees to follow. Create a safe environment to make sure kids feel comfortable expressing their thoughts and feelings and taking risks. If you know there is a particular child who will copy someone else's answer, have them answer first. Notice who is talking and who isn't, and try to make sure all voices are heard.

Example of a Group Agenda
Here's an example of how you could structure a group using this book:

- **Check-in** - How are you feeling today?

- **Topic of the Day -** Discussion about Listening

    o   What does it mean to listen?

    o   Are there times when it's easier to listen? How about when it's harder to listen?

- ○ What helps kids listen? What distracts kids from listening?
- ○ Can you think of a time when it would be good NOT to listen?

- **Mindful Listening Activity**

- **Debrief** - How did it go?
  - ○ What were your thoughts and/or feelings as you listened during the activity?
  - ○ When was it easy for you to listen? Why?
  - ○ When was it challenging to listen? Why?

- **Group Closing** – Share one good thing!

Have fun and enjoy your time with your groups!

CHAPTER 1
Listening

Listening is a fundamental skill, but it's tough to do! Listening includes hearing the words someone else is saying, understanding those words and then reacting appropriately to what they've said. It can be a challenge to listen carefully sometimes.

This can happen when we're by ourselves, like when we're watching a movie or listening to a book or podcast. We may get distracted by thoughts we have or something that moves in our peripheral vision. To accurately understand and process what we have heard, we need to be listening carefully.

Listening challenges can also happen when we're in a conversation with others. Sometimes when we're supposed to be listening, we are focused instead on what we want to say next rather than taking in what the other person is saying. If there are a group of people talking, this can make it even trickier to follow the conversation, listen, and respond appropriately.

If kids aren't listening well, they'll miss directions or important instructions in the classroom. Or may not quite get the funny punchline of a joke because they zoned out in the middle of it. Or they'll miss opportunities because they weren't listening to the details of what they are expected to do to earn certain experiences and opportunities.

Listening is a building block of other social skills, like taking another person's perspective, working together and solving problems. To take another person's perspective, you first have to hear them and listen to what they are saying to understand their point of view. When you're working on a team, everyone needs to be listening to everyone else to be successful and feel like everyone had a part in the project. The inability to listen to someone else, especially in scenarios where you may not agree on a tough topic, is a big reason for a lot of misunderstandings and unsolved conflicts. And to solve problems, no matter how big or small, the first step is to listen.

Introductory Discussion Questions

- What does it mean to listen?

- When is it important to listen?

- When you're by yourself, what's easy about listening? What's hard?

- When you're in a group, what's easy about listening? What's hard?

- Can you think of examples of when you saw someone listen? What happened?

- Can you think of examples of when you saw someone who didn't listen? What happened?

- Can you think of times when it would be good NOT to listen?

Stand Up Sit Down Game

The goal of the game is to have group members stand up when they hear a sentence that describes them. To participate successfully, the group members have to listen carefully and pay attention.

Materials Needed

Stand Up Sit Down Game handout (pg 12)

How to Play

Explain that when the group hears a sentence that describes them, they just stand up. Once you've said one statement, have everyone sit down again to reset. Then you read the next sentence.

To give you some starting ideas, I've created a handout with some questions. You can also use what you see in front of you to create sentences.

Other Ways to Play

Some kids may not be able to stand and sit. In that case, you can have kids raise hands or raise a certain color card to indicate their answers instead of standing and sitting.

Debrief Questions

- Did you find it easy or difficult to listen during this activity?
- Did that change as the game went on?
- What did you hear about the other members of the group?
- What sorts of things did you notice you have in common with other group members?
- How are you different from each other?
- What else would you like to learn about the other members of the group?

Stand Up Sit Down Game

- Stand up if you have brown eyes (blue eyes, hazel eyes, etc).

- Stand up if you have at least one sister (one brother, only child).

- Stand up if you have curly hair (brown hair, short hair, long hair, etc).

- Stand up if you have on the color blue (red, green, orange, etc).

- Stand up if you were born in Spring (Summer, Fall, Winter).

- Stand up if your favorite food is pizza (pasta, ice cream, etc).

- Stand up if you love chocolate (cookies, candy, etc).

- Stand up if you like reading (math, science, social studies).

- Stand up if you participate in a sport (basketball, soccer, lacrosse, etc).

- Stand up if you play an instrument (piano, violin, trumpet, etc).

- Stand up if you do an after-school activity (art club, karate, etc).

The Rain Game

Did you know you can make the sound of a rainstorm just with your fingers? This activity sounds amazing with a large or small group.

How to Play

Sit in a circle with your group. Direct the group members to pay attention to what the person on their right is doing, and as soon as they do an action, then they do it too. You start the action, and when it comes back around to you, start the next action. Go through the sequence like this:

- Rub thumb and forefinger together
- Rub hands together
- Snap fingers
- Clap hands
- Slap thighs
- Stomp feet
- Slap thighs
- Clap hands
- Snap fingers
- Rub hands
- Rub thumb and forefinger together
- Hands on lap

It should sound just like a rainstorm passing through, getting more intense, and then getting less intense. Such a neat listening activity!!

Other Ways to Play

If the group is really small (5 or less), do each of the actions 2 or 3 times to get a longer effect of each sound, as would happen in a bigger group.

Debrief Questions

- Did you think it sounded like a storm? Or did it sound like something else to you?

- What were your thoughts and/or feelings as you listened during the activity?

- When was it challenging to change your action (for example, from slapping thighs to clapping hands)?

- When was it easy for you to change your action (for example, from rubbing hands to snapping fingers)?

- If we did each of the actions together, how do you think that would that change the sound (you can even try it if you want!)?

Tell a Story

The goal of this activity is to create a story with each group member contributing a part of the story. This activity not only works on listening skills but also working together as a group. See what interesting, goofy, or zany stories they can make while using their powers of listening.

Materials Needed

Paper and pencil or whiteboard and markers (optional)

How to Play

The first person starts a story with one sentence. Then the next person adds to the story, and it continues until everyone has contributed at least one sentence to the story. (For smaller groups, you can go around two or three times.) Encourage group members to listen for details so they can add on to the story in a way that makes sense.

Other Ways to Play

- If you think it's going to be a challenge for kids to start the story, then you as the group leader can start the story yourself.

- To help, you can write down groups of words that they could use in the story to help them think creatively.

- If you think it's going to be too challenging for the group to keep track of the whole story, write the sentences down on paper or a board so everyone can see how the story is unfolding and help make connections to earlier parts of the story in their sentences.

Debrief Questions

- What was it like when it was your turn to create a sentence? Was it hard or easy to incorporate other things people before you said?

- What was easy about creating a story as a group? What was challenging?

- Is there anything you'd change about the story?

- Do you think you could add more to the story?

Mindful Listening Activity

This is a simple way to introduce mindfulness exercises to the group while using your sense of hearing. Mindfulness is being aware of what's happening in the present moment. It's not about trying to clear your mind, but allowing thoughts and emotions to come and go without judgment and familiarizing ourselves with the present moment. It takes practice to be able to do this. A great way to practice focusing on the present is to slow down and listen to the sounds all around that you didn't necessarily notice before.

Materials Needed

Listening ears

How to Play

Start by asking the group to get in a comfortable position in their chairs or on their carpet squares. They can close their eyes if they choose or they can keep them open. Have them take a few deep breaths. Then lead them through this listening exercise. Use a calm, soothing and gentle voice.

Say "Stretch your hearing outside where we are right now. What do you hear? Traffic from the street? Birds chirping? A garbage truck backing up?"

Wait a few minutes then say "Turn your attention to what's happening in this room where we are right now. What do you hear? Do you hear a sound machine? The lights buzzing? The clock ticking?"

Wait a few more minutes then say "Pay attention and listen to what's going on in your body. Can you hear your stomach rumbling? Do you have a headache?"

After a few minutes, encourage them to take a few deep breaths and open their eyes.

Other Ways to Play

Do this activity inside the room where you have group, and then maybe go to another area and do it again. What's the same? What's different?

Debrief Questions

- What were your thoughts and/or feelings as you listened during the activity?
- When was it easy for you to listen? Why?
- When was it challenging to listen? Why?

Begin with the End

This is a fun game that requires listening to words, then coming up with a word that starts with the letter they ended on.

Materials Needed

Imagination!

How to Play

Pick a group member to go first. That group member picks a word they want to start with and says it out loud. Then the next person listens carefully for the end letter and says a word that starts with that letter. For example, if the first person said the word "horse" then the second person needs to say a word that starts with "E" like "ear." Then the next person would say a word that starts with "R" like "right." Then the next person would say a word that begins with "T" like "tiger." This game can go on as long as you like!

Other Ways to Play

Want a challenge? Make it more complex by limiting the categories. Here are some ideas:

- Animals
- Foods
- Nouns
- Names
- Adjectives
- TV shows or movies

Debrief Questions

- What did you find easy about this game?
- What made this game more challenging?
- Did you ever get confused while you were listening? If so, how did you figure it out?

CHAPTER 2
Following Directions

Learning to follow directions is such a critical skill for positive social interactions. Kids need to be able to listen, internalize what they've heard, process it and then have their actions reflect what they've heard.

First and foremost, it's necessary for children to be able to follow the rules to stay safe. Some big examples include if they are crossing the street, or there's an emergency, and they need to get out of where they are, or there's something unsafe they need to avoid. It is of the utmost importance in these instances that children follow the directions.

The expectation that children will follow directions frequently occurs throughout their day. They're expected to be able to follow directions in the morning when it's time to get ready for school. They're expected to follow directions in class and throughout the school building during the school day. During after-school activities, like karate or soccer or dance or gymnastics, it's also expected that they will listen and follow the directions. Being able to listen and then follow directions will help these transitions go smoothly and help kids do what they need to do and be able to learn.

Children also need to follow directions when playing board games. To enjoy a game and play with others in an expected way, kids need to know and follow the rules of the game. When kids are playing a board game together, there's usually an expected set of rules. And while these rules can be flexible or can change, everyone has to be able to agree and follow the same directions for the game to be enjoyable.

Sometimes it would be advantageous **not** to follow the directions of someone. For instance, if a child is doing a creative art project, there may not be any directions. This sort of open-ended play helps kids with their flexibility and allows them to use their creative mind (and there are some of those in this book too!). Or, a more sinister example is perhaps a stranger is telling a child to come with him, and help him find his puppy - you don't want kids to follow those directions blindly.

No one is perfect 100% of the time. Both kids and grown-ups have a hard time following directions all of the time. Even if the activities don't turn out perfectly, they have practiced going through and following the directions.

Introductory Discussion Questions

- What does it mean to follow directions?

- When is it important to follow directions?

- What sort of directions do you follow at home? At school? At after-school activities?

- Can you think of examples of when you saw someone follow directions? What happened?

- Can you think of examples of when you saw someone who didn't follow directions? What happened?

- Can you think of times when it would be good NOT to follow directions?

Color and Create a Paper Airplane

A fun way to practice following directions and have a little playtime flying airplanes!

Materials Needed

- White 8.5 x 11 paper

- Crayons/markers/colored pencils

How to Play

- Give each child one piece of paper and have them draw on one side of the paper. Let them know they will be making paper airplanes later, but first, they are drawing to make each of their planes unique. They can draw patterns, blocks of colors, shapes, etc. Once they complete their drawing, then it's time to start turning that artwork into an airplane.

- Take that piece of paper and fold it in half lengthwise.

- Open it up again and bring the corners down to meet the crease in the middle (it makes two triangles).

- Take the corners of the small triangles and fold those in again to meet the crease in the middle.

- Now it's time to make the wings. Put the airplane on its side and fold one half down part way to make a wing. Repeat with the other side.

- Lift up the wings, and your plane is ready to fly!

Once your planes are done, of course, you have to test them! See how far everyone's planes go.

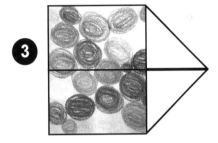
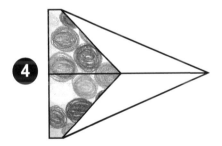
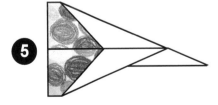
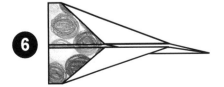

Make a target or a line on the ground to see if you can reach it.

Other Ways to Play

- Adjust folds on the airplanes to see if they will fly farther.

- Make different styles of airplanes to see which one flies the best.

- Feeling like you want to try some other paper airplanes? Check out Alex's Paper Airplanes site, complete with videos and instructions on how to make a large variety of airplanes and helicopters all out of paper.

Debrief Questions

- How did the experience of following the directions to make the paper airplane go for you?

- Have you ever followed different directions to make another type of paper airplane?

- What other items can you make by following directions?

Red Light, Green Light, Purple Light, Blue Light

This is a twist on the traditional red light, green light game. Group members follow directions that correspond to the different color lights.

Materials Needed

- A space big enough for your group to walk a short distance
- A start and a finish line

How to Play

Mark a start line and a finish line on the floor. One player is designated the leader and goes to stand at the finish line. The leader will call out the directions to other players. Then, the other players line up at the start line and follow the directions of the leader.

When the leader says **green light**, the players move as quickly as they can while being safe to the leader. When the leader calls out **red light**, the players stop. If the leader catches a player moving, then that player goes back to start. Whichever player reaches the leader first then gets to be the leader for the next round.

Add in different colors for different types of movement, for example:

- Purple Light = Skip
- Blue Light = Walk sideways
- Orange Light = Hop on one foot

Or use different colored lights to pretend to be different animals

- Yellow Light = Hop like a bunny
- Pink Light = Walk like an elephant
- Violet Light = Walk like a crab

Other Ways to Play

- Say words that rhyme with red and green to see if they catch the difference.
- Write which colors equal which movements in a visible place to make it easier for everyone to remember.

- Instead of the winner being the next leader, you can also have each child who is playing take turns being the leader.

Debrief Questions

- How did it feel to be the leader and give directions?

- How did it feel to be playing and following directions?

- Which did you find easier, giving or following directions?

Live Action Board Game

Your group members get a chance to play a real-life board game, and they are the pieces! This activity takes a bit more time to set up than other activities in this book, but the fun will be worth it.

Materials Needed

- Spinner, Start and Finish Markers, Action Boxes (pgs 27-30)

- Index cards, cardstock or some other way to mark each spot on the board game

- Metal brad

- Washi tape/masking tape (optional)

- Sidewalk chalk (optional)

How to Play

1. Set up the game board

    Figure out how you want your large board game to look. The game can be set up in a square or a circle or a squiggly line. Figure out what will work for the space that you have. If you desire, you can outline the game in washi tape or masking tape to make it look like a real board. Or if playing outside on a hardtop, make an outline in sidewalk chalk.

    To set up the game, copy and cut out the action cards and the start and finish markers, and place them on the index cards. These are your game spaces. Arrange these cards in your board game.

    There are 20 action items included here. You can adjust the length of your game by adding blank spaces in between every action item or making up your own action items to include.

2. Make the spinner

    Copy the spinner and arrow onto cardstock and cut it out. Line up the dots and then push the metal brad through the dot. Fold back the wings of the metal brad and your spinner is ready to use!

Once your group is ready to start, decide on what order kids will start the game in (oldest to youngest, youngest to oldest, shortest to tallest, who is wearing a certain color). Have kids move through the game and following the directions of the space where they land. Keep going until all players have finished the game.

Other Ways to Play

- While I've included action items to make it easier for you to set up, feel free to make your own.

- You can also encourage players to make their own and add them to the game too.

Debrief Questions

- How did it feel to be playing and following directions?

- What were your thoughts as you were following the different directions?

- How did you feel at the end of the game?

Start Here

Finish!

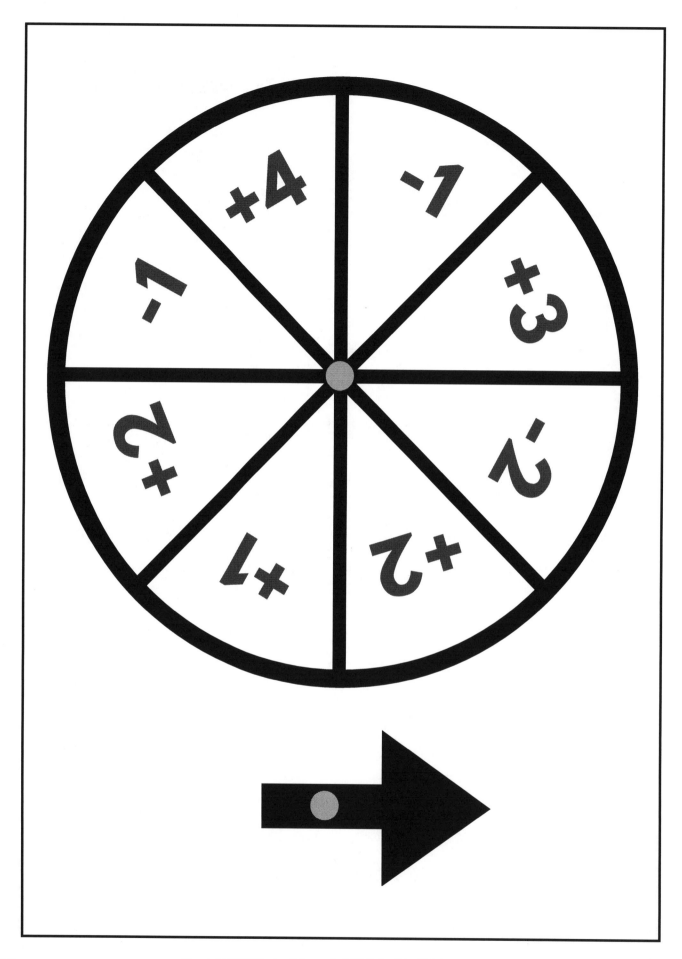

Make a fishy face	Meow like a kitty cat
Quack like a duck	Bark like a dog
Nay like a horse	Flap your arms like wings
Do a karate chop with your arms	Twirl like a ballet dancer
Disco dance	Hop like a bunny twice

Balance on one foot for 20 seconds	**Pat your head and rub your belly**
Touch your head, shoulders, knees and toes	**Touch your right hand to your left knee then switch**
Wiggle your fingers and toes	**Stand like a sumo wrestler**
Make a silly face	**Make circles with your arms**
Jump as high as you can	**Balance on your heels for 10 seconds**

Partner Drawing

This is an opportunity for group members to practice both following and giving directions.

Materials Needed

- Paper
- Markers/colored pencils/crayons

How to Play

Set group members up in pairs, and identify who will be giving the directions, and who will be drawing. The child who is giving directions tells their partner what to draw, what color paper to use and what colors to use. The drawing child does their best to follow the directions. Then after several minutes, have children switch roles.

Other Ways to Play

Give kids ideas of simple things to draw, like a rainbow and clouds or shapes, like a blue square, red heart, orange circle, purple diamond, black rectangle, etc.

Debrief Questions

- How was your experience following directions?
- How was your experience giving directions?
- Which did you find easier, giving or following directions?

Follow the Steps

The game starts out easily, with just one direction. It gets harder and harder the more directions you add in. See how far your group can get!

Materials Needed

The direction cards on pg 33.

How to Play

Copy and cut out the directions, and pick an order.

Have players stand up and give each other arm's length of room around them. Create a series of steps using the printable directions, starting with just one direction. Have players follow the directions. Then add more directions on, and see how many steps kids can remember. How many can they do and remember? Then rearrange the steps and start from the beginning.

For example:

- Wrinkle your nose

- Wrinkle your nose AND take three steps forward

- Wrinkle your nose AND take three steps forward AND touch your knees

Other Ways to Play

- Give each group member one direction, and have all the members do them in order. For example, player 1 takes three steps forward; player 2 hops backward one. The next player can't go until the previous movement is done.

- Each player gets their own set of directions, and every player starts at the same time and sees if they can focus on their moves and complete their sequences while others are doing a different series.

Debrief Questions

- When was it easy to follow the directions?

- When did it get challenging?

- Was there anything that helped you remember the directions as you went through?

Take 3 steps forward	**Do 3 jumping jacks**
Hop backwards once	**Touch your knees**
Wiggle your ears	**Wrinkle your nose**
Give yourself a hug	**Stand on one foot**
Put your hands on your head	**Tap your toes**
Put your hands on your hips	**Stick out your tongue**

Problem-Solving

Problem-solving is an important skill to have to manage small everyday issues and bigger life concerns. Kids face problems all the time, but sometimes they get stuck and don't know how to figure out what to do to solve it. A kid could have forgotten their lunch money, and not know what to do next. Or a kid could get into an argument with another kid over a game at recess. Practicing this skill now will help later when they are faced with bigger decisions as they move into adulthood. Problem-solving actually involves several steps.

Identify the Problem

First, they need to get a good understanding of the problem they are facing. Sometimes kids will identify one thing as the problem, but it turns out to be something else. It's important to make sure they understand the situation and clarify the specific problem.

Help kids figure out the size of a problem. Is this a small problem, a medium-sized problem or a big problem? Here's a good way to divide it up:

Small - You can solve it by yourself easily in a few minutes.

Medium - You need an adult and/or the problem takes a little longer to solve.

Big - You need to call 911, or you need an adult to help you, and it will take several hours or days to fix it.

Knowing the size of the problem will have an impact on the steps they take to solve it - can I work on fixing this problem myself or do I need help from someone else?

Generate Ideas

They need to be able to generate several ideas for solving an issue. Not all of them will work, but you're not trying to pick out ones that will and won't work during this step. During this step, it's just about generating ideas.

Evaluate Ideas

Go through each of the suggestions generated and figure out which ideas are ones to try and which ones to leave behind.

Decide on a Solution and Try It

Pick an idea for solving the problem and give it a try.

Did It Work?

After you've tried to solve the problem, check in to see if it worked. If it did, awesome! If it didn't, just go back and pick another solution that you thought of during the "Evaluate Ideas" step and see if that works.

5 Steps to Solving a Problem

1. Identify the Problem

Sometimes kids will identify one thing as the problem, but it really turns out to be something else. Make sure you understand the situation and clarify the specific problem.

2. Generate Ideas

Generate several ideas for solving an issue. Not all of them will work, but you're not trying to pick out ones that will and won't work during this step. Just generate as many ideas as you can.

3. Evaluate Ideas

Go through and figure out which ideas are ones to try and which ones to leave behind.

4. Decide on a Solution and Try it

Pick an idea for solving the problem and give it a try

5. Did it work?

After you've tried to solve the problem, check in to see if it worked. If it did, awesome! If it didn't, just go back and pick another solution that you thought of during step 3.

Introductory Discussion Questions

- What sorts of small problems do kids have at school? Medium-sized problems? Large problems?

- What sorts of small problems would kids have at home? Medium-sized problems? Large problems?

- Have you ever had a problem that you solved on your own? Please share!

- Have you ever had a problem and gotten help to fix it? Please share!

- What do you think is the hardest part of solving a problem?

Creative Problem-Solving Prompts

This is a fun way to use everyday materials and unique prompts to practice solving problems.

Materials Needed

- Problem-solving prompts (pg 40)
- Paper straws
- Cotton balls
- Yarn
- Paper cups
- Clothespins
- White cord
- Tape
- Popsicle sticks
- Paper clips
- Sticky notes

(Feel free to substitute if you don't have something. This is meant to be easy to set up, not extra work for you!)

How to Play

Explain to the group that they are going to practice solving problems. Go through the printable sheet of problems together, and choose a problem to tackle as a group. Explain to your group that they can use any of the ten materials in front of them to solve the problem. They don't have to use all the materials, but they are all available to them. Encourage group members to use the problem-solving steps to figure out what to do.

If there is time left over once the first problem has been solved, they can go back and pick another one.

Other Ways to Play

Before group begins, you pick out the problems that the group will be solving.

Debrief Questions

- How did you decide which problems to solve?
- What role did different group members play during these challenges?
- How did the group work together?
- What worked well?
- What didn't work as well?

Make a device to move a stuffed animal from one room to another without touching the ground	Devise a slide for mini figures
Make a leprechaun trap	Create a jump ramp for cars
Use at least 4 supplies, build the highest tower you can	Make up your own game - make sure you remember to make rules for how to score and win
Make a device for two people to communicate to one another	Using at least 3 supplies, make a device that can roll 3 feet
Build a house for a small figure	Make an invention that a kid would love

Newspaper Tower Challenge

This activity can set you up for some fantastic teachable moments so be prepared. The object of the activity is to build a tower out of newspaper and tape that can stand up on its own without leaning on other items in the room.

Materials Needed

- Newspaper

- Masking tape/scotch tape

How to Play

Give the group access to the materials and set a timer (perhaps 10 - 15 minutes). Group members need to cooperate, work together, and problem solve to build a tower.

Other Ways to Play

- Have the group compete against themselves. Have the group do the activity once, then have them do it again and see if they can improve on their structure.

- Challenge play: Divide the group in two, and have them compete to see who can build the highest tower.

- Challenge play: Take away the tape and see how high they can build their structures.

Debrief Questions

- What were the problems you faced when building the tower?

- How did the group problem solve?

- What role did different group members play in creating the tower?

Make a Solution Wheel

When kids have a conflict, sometimes they don't always know what to do. In the moment, they can't remember things that they can do to help work through a problem. A solution wheel is a great visual resource to help remind them of different ways to solve a problem. One of the reasons I do like this lesson is because it's working on solving problems AND it's a craft project.

The group members can use their solution wheel in the group with you to solve a few problems, and then they can take it home and use it there too.

Materials Needed

- Solution Wheel and Arrow handout (pg 44)

- Construction paper/cardstock paper

- Metal brad

- Glue

How to Play

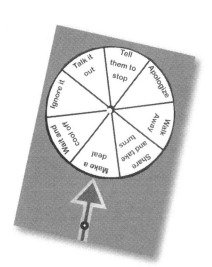

- Have the kids pick a color of construction paper they want to use, then cut out the solution wheel and an arrow.

- Glue the arrow to the bottom of the piece of construction paper, having the bottom of the arrow line up with the bottom of the construction paper.

- Connect the solution wheel to the construction paper using a metal brad so it can spin.

Now it's ready to use! Use the solution wheel to help group members figure out what they could do in these different situations:

- Two kids are arguing over which game to play at recess. What could you do?

- You are getting frustrated with your little brother's behavior. What could you do?

- You are walking over to use a swing, then someone runs in front of you and takes it first. What can you do?

- You bump into someone, and their books fall out of their hands. What can you do?

- Someone says something that makes you mad. What can you do?

Note: Let your group members know this is not a type of wheel that you just spin, wait for the wheel to land, and use that solution. You turn it until you find a solution you want to try. Also, make sure to let them know that the solution wheel can't solve every problem all the time, but it is a good place to start especially with small or medium-sized problems.

Other Ways to Play

- Have kids suggest current problems that are happening during the school day or at home to try and solve using the solution wheel.

- You can also keep this wheel in your room/office and use it as a reference point when children are having a problem. Use suggestions from the solution wheel to help brainstorm ways to work on fixing the problem.

Debrief Questions

- What other solutions can you think of that aren't on the solution wheel?

- Have you seen anyone have a problem recently, like at recess or on the bus? What did they do? Which solutions would have worked in that situation?

- Can you give examples of problems that couldn't be solved by using a solution wheel?

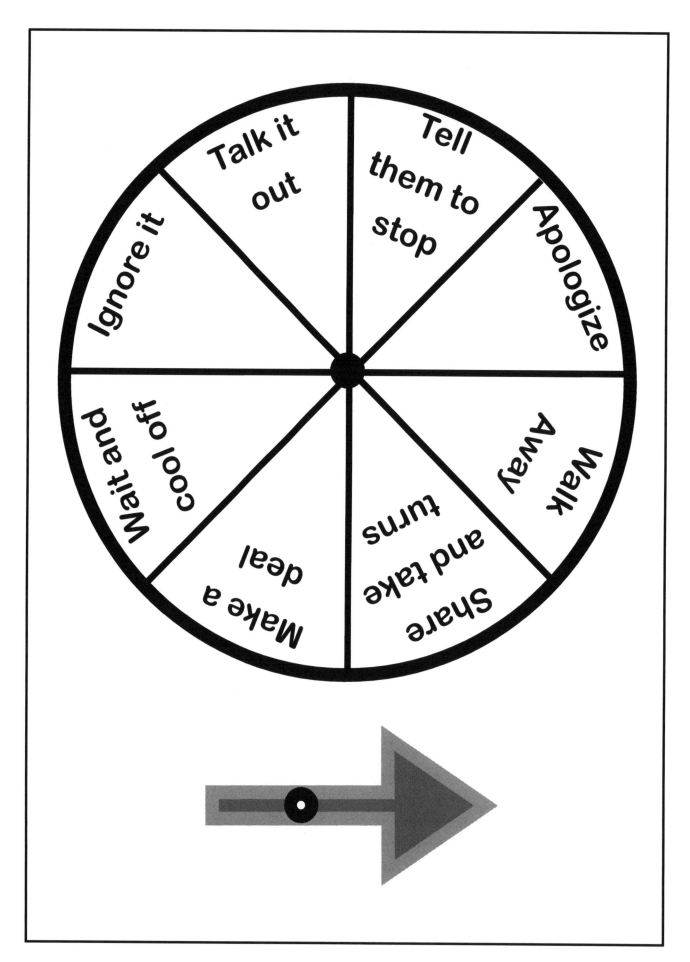

Make a Maze with Straws

Here's a fun problem for your group to solve together: make a maze using cardboard, straws, and tape. The goal is to have an item, like a marble, complete the maze from start to finish. By taping straws inside the cardboard box, the group can make a maze through which they can send items.

Materials Needed

- Big cardboard with a raised edge (the top of a box, or a box cut down)
- Straws
- Tape
- Pom poms, marbles, tiny spiky ball or a HEXBUG®

How to Play

First, as a group, they need to figure out which item they want to get through the maze. Next, they plan out the route, including dead ends. Then they can cut, bend and tape the straws as needed to create the paths. Once they've completed making the maze, they can send their chosen item through.

Other Ways to Play

- Use the maze with one type of item, then try another. For example, if you used a marble, try having a HEXBUG go through the maze. Does it still work?
- Use pom poms and straws and take turns blowing the pom pom through the maze from start to finish.
- Use LEGOs® and a LEGO baseplate (or DUPLOs® and a DUPLO baseplate), to create a maze for marbles, spiky balls, or pom poms.

Debrief Questions

- What types of problems did you run into when you were doing this project? How did you solve them?
- Did the maze work the first time you tried it? If not, how did you solve that problem?
- What was the easiest part of this activity?
- What was the most challenging part of this activity?
- If you could do it over again, what would you change?

Paper Plate Challenge

The goal is to get the whole group from the start line across the finish line only stepping on paper plates. The group has to problem solve to figure out how to accomplish this.

Materials Needed

- Paper plates - enough for everyone in the group plus one

- Tape or cones to mark start and finish lines

Before the Activity

Mark a start and a finish line in your group space.

How to Play

Give every person in the group one paper plate, and give the group one extra paper plate. The only rules are that you cannot touch the ground with your feet, and you have to move forward on the paper plates. Every person has to cross the finish line for the activity to be complete.

Other Ways to Play

You can time the group to see how long it takes them to get from start to finish. Then, once they've figured out a way to get across, time them again to see if they improved.

If they are struggling, give them this hint: They can pass paper plates to one another!

Debrief Questions

- How did you figure out the problem of getting from start to finish just using paper plates?

- When you started, what did you think of the problem?

- After you figured it out, what did you think of the problem?

- What worked well?

- What were the challenges?

- What were your thoughts and feelings as you were doing this challenge?

- If you could do it over again, what would you change?

CHAPTER 4

Flexibility

What does flexibility mean? In the context of social skills, it's not about being physically flexible, but more about being flexible in your thinking. When kids are flexible, they tend to do better in social situations. It makes other people feel good, and other kids want to be around a kid who is flexible.

Some kids struggle with rigid thinking. They may have a set idea in their mind of how things are supposed to go, and they don't react well if that exact plan doesn't happen. They can experience what is known as "all or nothing thinking," where you view things in black and white, and can't see the gray. However, in real life, there is gray. Plans change. People are late, or things get canceled. Kids need to learn to be flexible, think outside of the box and manage changes. Being flexible for these kids means being willing to change plans and go with the flow. It means looking at things a different way. It means letting go of being in charge and being super strict about the rules of games all the time.

Let's not forget about kids who are too flexible. They let everyone else go first all the time, they let others pick which color they want to be every game, and they never say what they want. Sure, this kid is great to have in group or class because they don't make waves, but they're also never asserting their desires and wishes. They need to work on standing up for themselves.

The goal is balance - ideally, we want kids who aren't too rigid but also aren't too flexible. There should be a balance in their flexibility, not too much and not too little.

Introductory Discussion Questions

- What does it mean to be flexible?

- What does it mean to be a flexible thinker or a flexible person?

- When is it easy to be flexible?

- When is it hard to be flexible?

- Can you give examples of times when people have been inflexible?

- Can you give examples of times when people are too flexible?

- Is it easier to be flexible at home? At school? At after-school activities?

Invitation to Create

Invite your group members to use their originality and resourcefulness as they use materials with different flexibility to create whatever they want. This lesson creates a visual demonstration of flexibility and encourages creative thinking!

Materials Needed

- Pipe cleaners
- Yarn
- Popsicle sticks
- Beads

How to Play

Encourage your group members to use their flexible mind and create anything they want with these items. It could be a person, a creature, a structure or anything else they can think of that they could make. Set a timer and see what the group members create with these materials.

Other Ways to Play

- Have them create with only yarn and beads, then popsicle sticks and beads, then finally pipe cleaners and beads.
- Work in pairs or as a group to create something with the materials.

Debrief Questions

- What did you create?
- How flexible were the first three materials (yarn, popsicle sticks, pipe cleaners)?
- How did the yarn work with the beads? How did the popsicle sticks work? The pipe cleaners? Which did you prefer to use? Which one was the easiest to use? Which one was the hardest?
- When did you use flexible thinking during this activity?
- Wrap-up: Explain that each of the first three materials represents how flexible people can be. Some people can be too rigid, like the popsicle sticks. Some people can be too soft, like yarn. People who are like pipe cleaners are flexible but still strong. Try to aim for being flexible and strong like that.

Flexible Thinking with Silly Putty

Did you know that when you draw with a pencil and put silly putty on top of the drawing, a copy of the drawing goes onto the putty? Use that experience to discuss flexible thinking!

Materials Needed

- Silly Putty® (one for each member of the group) - lighter colors work best

- Pencils

- Thinking Bubbles (pg 52)

How to Play

Make copies of the thinking bubble printable for each member of the group. Use the thinking bubbles printable to discuss inflexible thoughts kids may have.

Start with the example bubbles, like the "I hate spinach" bubble. Discuss flexible ways to think about that statement. Once kids can come up with a way to think more flexibly, then take silly putty and put it over the bubble. Press down and peel it off. Point out to the group that the silly putty picks up the print from the page. Stretch the silly putty out and show how flexible your thinking can be!

With the blank bubbles, have kids write down an example of a thought they've seen other kids get stuck on. Once they figure out a way to be flexible about that thought, then they can put the silly putty over the bubble, peel it off and stretch it out. Look how flexible your thoughts can be!

Other Ways to Play

- Have kids cross off the inflexible thought and write in the flexible thought in the bubble and then use the silly putty to stretch it out.

- Divide the group into pairs to work on thinking of more flexible thoughts.

- Before group begins, you as the group leader identify a few major inflexible thoughts that are common among the group members. Use the blank bubble sheet to write those in, and work together as a whole group to think of other ways to be more flexible.

Debrief Questions

- Was it easy or challenging to come up with flexible ways to think?

- Were certain questions easier than others? Why?

- Can you give an example of a time when someone changed from inflexible to flexible thinking?

New Rules for Old Games

Part of being flexible means being able to do things differently. Take games that the group is familiar with and change up the rules to practice doing things differently.

Materials Needed

- Board or card games
- Imagination to create different rules

How to Play

Work as a group and create different rules for these well-known games. Some examples:

- Instead of Connect 4®, play connect 3 or connect 5.
- Instead of UNO®, play Dos or Nada.
- Play war and the player who wins is the one who doesn't have any cards at the end.
- Instead of Crazy 8's®, play Crazy 6's.

Then it's time to play! See how it goes as you're playing by different rules.

Other Ways to Play

- Some games, like Sorry®, have changed their rules over the years. If you can, find older versions of the rules that you can use to play by.
- Play by the original rules of the game first, then change it up and play by the new rules you created.
- Divide the group in two and have multiple games going at once.

Debrief Questions

- Did you prefer the old or the new rules? Why?
- What was easy about playing by different rules? What was challenging?
- How does playing by different rules relate to being flexible?
- Is this something you'd try at home or with other friends? What would be the challenges of doing that?

Think Outside the Box

This is a fun way for kids to look at an everyday item, and think about it differently. What will they create?

Materials Needed

- Cardboard box
- Ribbon
- Tape
- Glue
- Scissors
- Construction paper
- Straws
- Paint/markers

How to Play

Place a box in the middle of the table. Instruct them that this is, in fact, not a box. They are in charge of figuring out what this item is. They can use their imagination and create whatever they can think of using the materials in front of them. Some ideas to get them started:

- Rocketship
- Dollhouse
- Puppet Theater
- Aquarium
- Dragon
- Car garage
- Boat
- Train
- Treasure chest
- Robot

Other Ways to Play

- Give each student their own small cardboard box to use for creating.
- Divide the group into pairs or smaller teams to work on creating something together.

Debrief Questions

- What did you end up creating? How did you come up with the idea?
- How does "thinking outside the box" relate to flexible thinking?
- Have you ever done anything like this before? Do you remember what you created?

Combine and Play

Playing with one type of toy can encourage flexible thinking, but those flexible thinking strategies are pushed further when kids play with two different types of toys, especially ones they've never combined before.

Materials Needed

Two open-ended toys (a toy that can be played with in many different ways). Here are some suggestions:

- Toy cars
- LEGO/DUPLO bricks
- Blocks
- KEVA Planks®
- K'NEX®
- Magna-Tiles®
- Dolls
- Small figures (like from TOOBS® containers)
- Art & craft supplies (markers, crayons, construction paper, scissors, etc.)
- Cardboard
- Connectagons®
- Dominoes
- Cash register/pretend money

How to Play

Lay out two different types of toys/items on the table. Tell the group that they need to figure out to play with these items together. Some ideas to get you started:

- Combine art supplies and LEGOs to create a city
- Combine cars and pretend money to create a garage
- Combine dolls and KEVA blocks to create a doll hospital
- Combine Magna-Tiles and K'NEX to make a creature

Other Ways to Play

- Start with two types of toys then add in a third, or fourth!
- Start with three or four types of toys.
- Have the group choose the two toys they'll be using during group.

Debrief Questions

- What did you end up making and/or playing? How did you come up with the idea?
- How was it combining different types of toys?
- Can you share how you were flexible in your thinking during this activity?

CHAPTER 5
Working Together

Working together means being able to collaborate with other people on a specific goal. But it can be a challenge to do that! There are several different social skills needed to work successfully as a group. Kids need to be able to listen to others' ideas and compromise about which ideas to pursue. Every person has to do their part when working as a group. It's not very much fun nor is it fair to other group members when everyone doesn't do their share of the work.

A lot more emphasis is being placed on the importance of group work in school nowadays. For kids to be successful students, they need to learn how to work together to accomplish the project or assignment given to them by the teacher.

Not only is it a good skill to know how to use during school, but it's also a good skill to have for the future too. Often, when you are working at a job, you may need to collaborate with others, learn to listen to other people's ideas, be flexible and work together to accomplish a goal.

Introductory Discussion Questions

- What makes it easy for people to work together?

- What makes it challenging for people to work together?

- Have you ever had to work on a group project? How did that go?

- If you were working on a group project, and one person did not do their assigned part, how would you feel? What would you think?

- When do you need to work together at school?

- When do you need to work together at home?

- Can you give examples of people working together to accomplish a goal?

Make a Working Catapult

This is a fun way to practice working together. It may not go smoothly the first time, which is the perfect opportunity for teachable moments to occur. Use these teachable moments and encourage kids to problem solve and work together.

Materials Needed

- Popsicle sticks - 5 for 1 catapult
- Rubber band
- One small cup for the catapult
- Stack of cups for the tower
- Hot glue gun
- Ping pong balls/pom poms/cotton balls

How to Play

Prep Popsicle Catapult

(NOTE: you can do the hot glue parts before group begins, so you don't have to worry about having a glue gun on when group is happening)

- Start making catapult by gluing three popsicle sticks together in a stack.
- Hot glue gun one cup to the end of one popsicle stick (save the last popsicle stick for when you put it all together).

Put Together Catapult

- Stack (don't glue!) the popsicle stick with the cup on top of the remaining popsicle stick. Tie the rubber band around these two sticks at the opposite end of the cup.
- Place the stack of 3 popsicle sticks in between the two popsicle sticks that are wrapped together with a rubber band. The stick with the cup attached should be on the top, like this picture.

- Set up Target: Use the cups to set up a cup tower.
- Aim and Fire the Ping Pong Balls: Kids can work together to aim their catapults at the target to knock it down.
- Assign different kids in the group to either work on the catapult or work on setting up the target. Then the catapult group will have to work together to aim the catapult and get the pom poms to fire and knock down the tower. The tower group has to work together to create the paper cup structure that's going to be knocked down by the catapult group.

Other Ways to Play

- Have the group do the project one way, then have the group members switch roles (those who worked on the catapult now switch to setting up the target, and those who worked on setting up the target now work on the catapult).
- Have the whole group work on creating the catapult, then have the whole group set up the tower. Each member takes a turn using the catapult to knock down the tower.
- If your group is big enough, make multiple catapults and multiple cup towers.
- If you have big popsicle sticks, then use five to make the stack for the catapult.

Debrief Questions

- Overall, how did you all work together?
- What went well?
- What was a challenge?
- If you did this activity again, what would you change about how you worked?

To see a video of a catapult in action, visit encourageplay.com/videos

Make a Balloon Rocket

The object of this activity is to get a balloon from one side of your group space to the other. Again, this is an activity that will probably not go smoothly the first time, which is the perfect teachable moment.

Materials Needed

- Straws cut into 1" - 2" pieces
- Parachute cord or rope or string that will fit through the straw
- Balloons (one for everyone in the group)
- Tape

How to Play

Tape a piece of straw to the balloon. String the parachute cord through the straw. Then find an area with some room. You'll need two group members to hold either side of the string. One should hold the balloon, and one side of the string on one end of the space and the other should hold the other end of the string. The group member holding the side with the balloon should blow up the balloon, then let it go. See how far across the room it will go! Experiment with how to hold the string or how big to blow up the balloon and what impact that has on the balloon's trajectory.

Other Ways to Play

- Before you let go of the balloon, make a guess about how it will go. Did it beat your estimation?
- Have two balloons race at the same time and see which one wins!

Debrief Questions

- Did the balloon rockets work as you thought they would? If they didn't, what changes did you make to make them work?
- What went well?
- What was a challenge?
- If you did this activity again, what would you change about how you worked?

To see a video of a balloon rocket in action, visit encourageplay.com/videos

Treasure Hunt

I love to set up treasure hunts because they're a lot of fun. But did you know you can use them to help kids work on social skills? It's a great way to have kids not only work together, but also practice picking up on clues, taking turns, and problem-solving.

There are ten clues in all. There are two clues per page, and the clues have been numbered to make it easier for you. This activity requires a bit more set up, but it's worth it!

Materials Needed

- Treasure Hunt (pgs 63-68)
- "Treasure" for group to find at the end of the hunt

Before Group

To set up the treasure hunt for the kids, you need to:

- Think about where you will be placing the clues. Make it as easy or as hard as you think your group can handle. You can place it out in the open so they can easily see it, or you can hide it in a less obvious place, like behind a door or under an item.

- Write where to find the clues. There is a space on each clue to write the location of the **next** clue. This is the trickiest part of setting up the treasure hunt. I recommend writing on each clue as you place them, so you don't get confused.

- Place the prize - For the last clue, have them find a "treasure." It could be items from a prize box. Or it could be something like a puzzle they get to complete as a group.

How to Play

Give the kids the "START THE TREASURE HUNT" paper and watch the fun begin! Encourage them to work together to figure out where to look and make smart guesses about their "treasure." Feel free to step in and help if they get stuck.

Other Ways to Play

- Add in little treasures with each clue as they go along. For example, if the end of the treasure hunt is a puzzle, tape pieces of the puzzle to the clues to make it more interesting.

- Add in words on the clues that make a sentence that will reveal what they will receive as a treasure at the end.

- To make it even more challenging, put letters on the clues, then they have to unscramble the word/phrase to figure out the treasure.

Debrief Questions

- What went well during the treasure hunt? Was it easy or challenging to find the clues?

- What were some of the challenges?

- What were your thoughts and feelings when you completed the treasure hunt?

- If you did this activity again, what would you change about how you worked together?

To see a video of how to set up the treasure hunt, visit encourageplay.com/videos

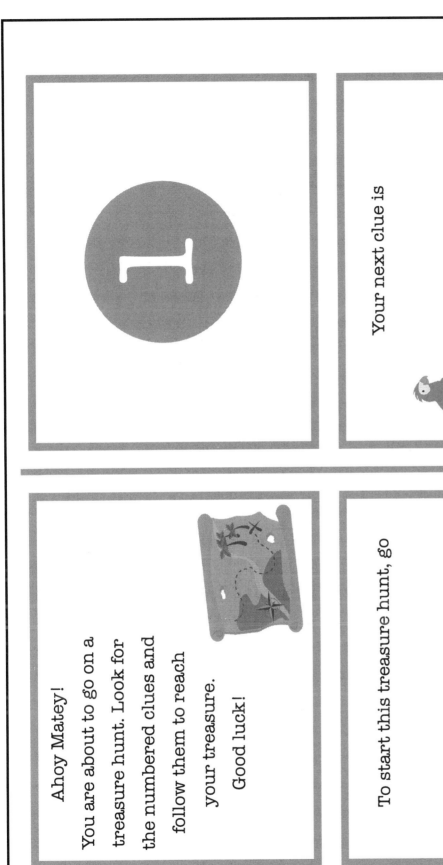

1

Ahoy Matey!
You are about to go on a treasure hunt. Look for the numbered clues and follow them to reach your treasure.
Good luck!

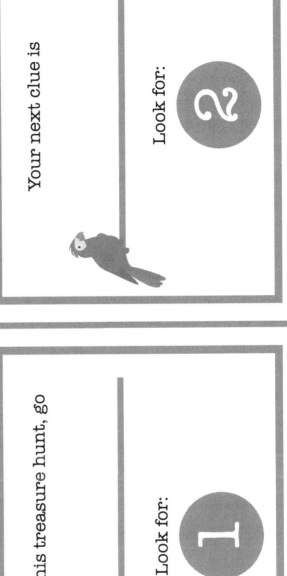

Your next clue is

Look for:

2

To start this treasure hunt, go

Look for:

1

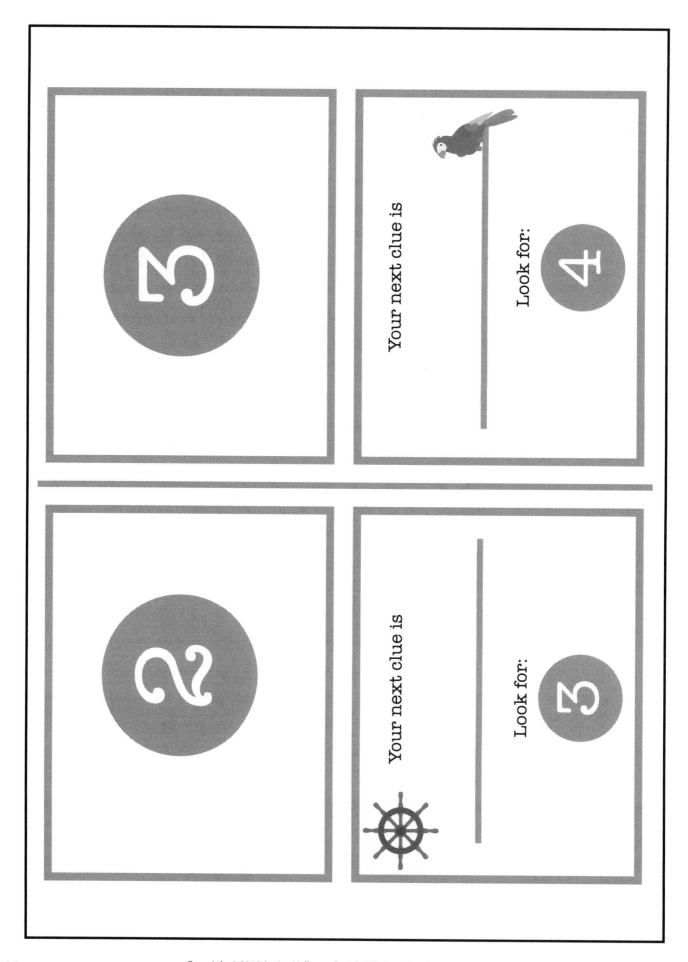

3

Your next clue is

_____

Look for:

4

2

Your next clue is

_____

Look for:

3

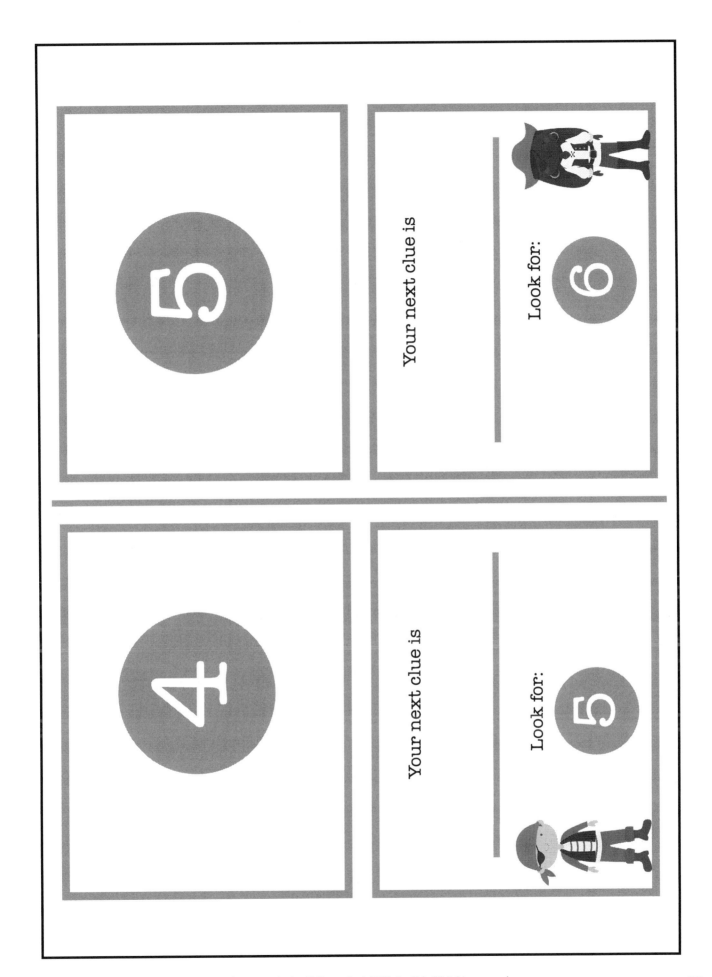

5

Your next clue is

Look for: 6

4

Your next clue is

Look for: 5

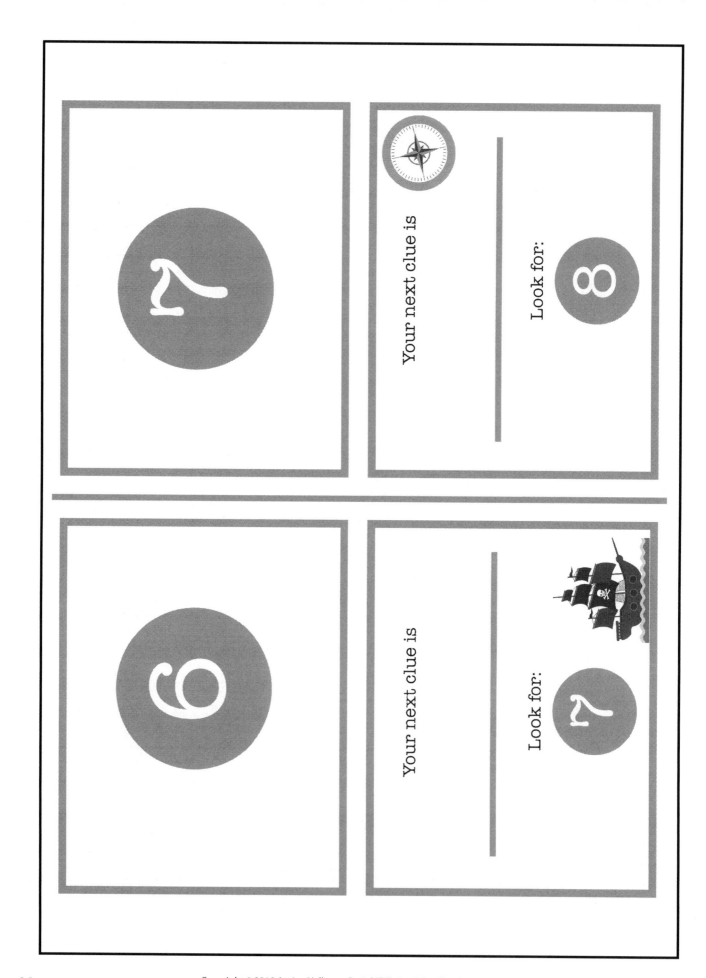

7

Your next clue is

_____

Look for:

8

9

Your next clue is

_____

Look for:

7

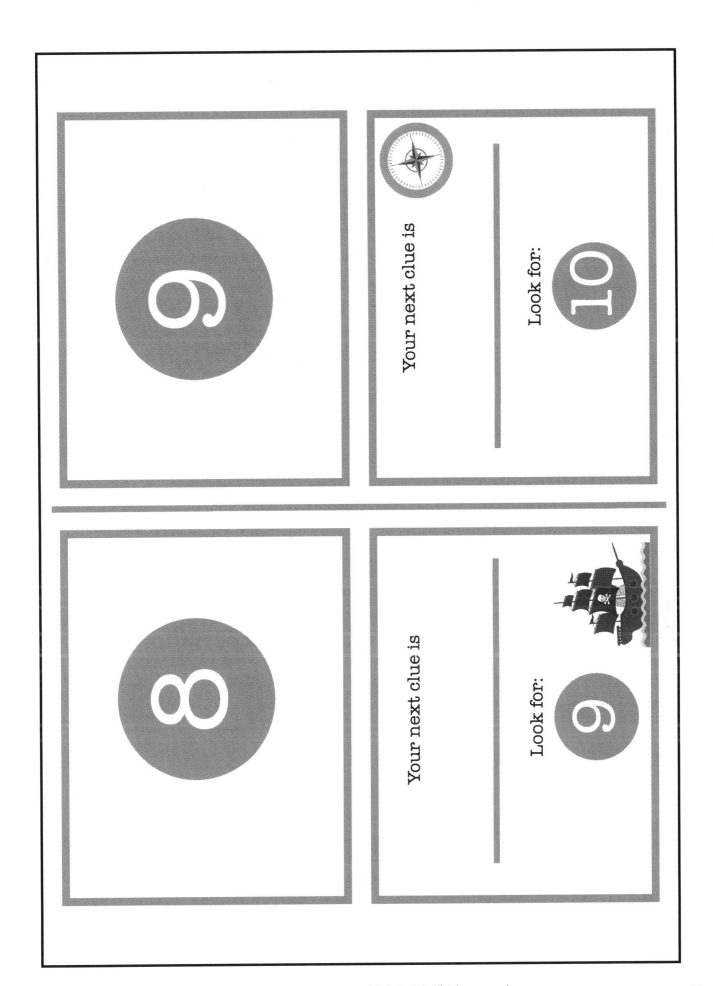

7

Your next clue is

_____

Look for:

10

8

Your next clue is

_____

Look for:

9

10

You're almost there! Look

and claim your treasure, arrrr!

Stack the Cups

It sounds easy - we stacked cups in the Make a Working Catapult activity earlier in this chapter. But the trick of this activity is that the group members can't use their hands. The only materials they can use to move the cups are rubber bands and string. They need to coordinate their movements and pulling the rubber band to stack the cups as a group.

Materials Needed

- String
- Cups
- Rubber band small enough to fit around cups

How to Play

Cut out one piece of string for each person in a group. Attach the strings to a rubber band so that the string is evenly spaced around the entire rubber band.

Challenge the group to stack 6 cups into a pyramid (three on the bottom, two on the middle row, and one on top) using only the string and rubber band to move and stack the cups. They have to work together and communicate to make the pyramid happen.

Other Ways to Play

- Depending on the size of your group, you can divide the group in two for this activity.

- Time them to see if they can improve their stacking skills.

- Have them use 10 cups instead of 6 to make a taller pyramid.

- Instead of using cups to stack, attach the rubber band to a marker and have them write one word as a group.

Debrief Questions

- How did you work together as a group?

- What were your thoughts and feelings when you finally finished the tower?

- If you did this activity again, what would you change about how you worked together?

Keep the Ball Up

This is a simple activity that is a great opportunity for everyone to work together as a group. It doesn't require any advanced preparation, and there are lots of other ways to play that you can add in. Try the activity the original way, then add in some of the other varieties too!

Materials Needed

- Beach ball (more than one, if you can)
- Space (move chairs and desks out of the way)

How to Play

The object of the game is for the group members to work together to keep a beach ball up in the air without touching the ground for one minute. Members need to stay aware and work together to keep the ball in the air by hitting it to other members of the group. Once the minute starts and the ball is in the air, count how many times the ball is touched. If the ball falls before one minute is up, start again. If you make it, try to beat how many times the ball was touched during that first round the second time you play.

Other Ways to Play

- Try the activity for 2 or 3 minutes, or even longer!
- Add another ball, and see if the group can keep two balls going at the same time.
- When you hit the ball, call out the name of the person you're passing it to. If the person you called doesn't get it, you have to start over.
- Choose an order for the group to touch the ball and see how many times they can do it without touching the ground. Want a tough challenge? Switch up where members of the group are standing and try it again. Want an even tougher challenge? Add another ball!

Debrief Questions

- How did you work together as a group?
- If you tried other ways to play, which was your favorite?
- Which way was the easiest? The most challenging?
- If you did this activity again, what would you change about how you worked together?

CHAPTER 6

Taking Turns

Children (and people in general) take turns all the time. Children take turns not only when they play games like checkers or foursquare, but also while they participate in a class discussion, or when they're having a conversation at recess or in the bus line.

It's good to practice turn-taking, because it will be a social skill that will be used on a daily basis, not only as children but also as adults. Adults have to wait and take turns too - in meetings, in stores and when driving.

There are two major parts to taking turns. The first part happens when it is your turn - that tends to be pretty easy. You get to share your thoughts, take your turn in a game, or do what you want to do. But taking turns also involves waiting when it **isn't** your turn. That can be frustrating for kids. These games are designed to help kids enjoy the moment when it is their turn and practice waiting when it's not their turn to play.

Introductory Discussion Questions

- Can you give examples of when kids have to take turns?

- Can you give examples of when grown-ups have to take turns?

- Think about what you've done today. How many times have you taken turns today?

- What's easy about taking turns?

- What's hard about taking turns?

- What helps you when you're waiting to take your turn?

DIY Memory Game

Kids practice taking turns in this activity not only when they are making the memory pieces (they have to wait for the scissors or wait for a certain color marker to be available). They also practice taking turns when they are playing their DIY Memory Game together.

Materials Needed

- Construction paper

- Scissors*

- Colored pencils, markers or crayons*

  * Not every member of the group to needs to have their own

How to Play

Have each group member take one piece of construction paper, and fold it in half lengthwise, then in half again. Then fold it widthwise in half, then in half again. There should be 16 rectangles. Cut along the folded lines. Group members will be taking turns with scissors.

Have each group member draw the same image on two different pieces of construction paper. You can keep it simple like squares, triangles, hearts, moons, suns. Or get more creative, drawing patterns or pictures. Group members have to share and take turns with the colored pencils, markers or crayons. Be creative and have fun - just make sure both images look the same! When they are done, they should have eight pairs of images.

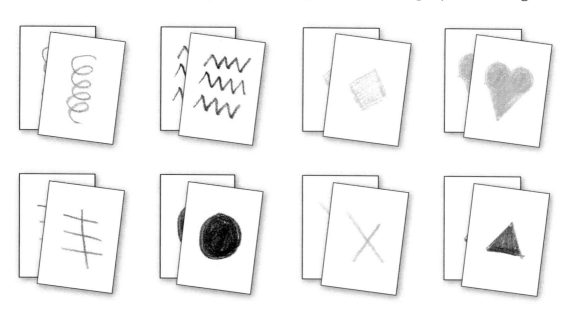

Then, have the group break out into pairs and using both of their sets of DIY Memory Game, they can play together.

- Turn over all the pieces - mix them up, so the pairs aren't next to each other!

- Decide who will go first.

- Players take turns trying to find the pairs. On your turn, turn over two squares. If the squares are the same, you keep the pair. If you find a pair, you get another turn. If you don't find a pair, it's your partner's turn.

- Keep going until all the pairs are found. The person with the most pairs wins!

Other Ways to Play

- If you think it will be too challenging for the group members to take turns while they create their games, then provide enough scissors and drawing materials.

- Another way to make it a little easier, choose only one supply to limit - provide enough scissors for the group, but not drawing materials, or vice versa.

- To make it even easier, cut out the construction paper before so the group can just concentrate on drawing.

Debrief Questions

- How did it go with sharing supplies while you were creating your games?

- How did taking turns go while you were playing memory?

- Was there anything that made it easier for you to wait for your turn?

Make a Crazy Creature

Group members take turns and make a crazy looking creature!

Materials Needed

- Crazy Creature handout (pg 76) - copy 1 for every 2 group members

- One die

- Pencils, colored pencils, crayons or markers

- Paper

How to Play

Divide your group into pairs.

- Pick one player to go first.

- That player rolls the die and draws the corresponding image on a separate piece of paper. That player keeps going, rolling the die and drawing an image until they've gone through all the columns and they have a completed crazy creature.

Then the die and game board are passed to the other person, who takes their turn and draws a complete picture.

Other Ways to Play

Instead of one person in the pair drawing their entire crazy creature, they can take turns as they go through each column:

- One person rolls the die to figure out what shape to use from the first column.

- The die and game board are passed to the other person, who takes their turn to find out what shape to draw from the second column.

- The die and board are handed back to the first person, who then rolls to figure out what to draw from the next column.

- Keep going back and forth until both people are done with all columns.

Debrief Questions

- How did it go with sharing the board game and die as you made your crazy creature?

- Was there anything that made it easier for you to wait for your turn?

- What was the most challenging part of this activity? What was the easiest?

	First Roll: Body	Second Roll: Eyes	Third Roll: Legs	Fourth Roll: Mouth

Group Drawing

Doing a group drawing is a wonderful way to build group cohesion, and a great way to practice taking turns! This activity allows for lots of creativity - there are different ways to approach a drawing as a group. Figure out the one that will work best for you and your group! Perhaps even try a few different ways.

Materials Needed

- Huge poster board/paper

- 8.5 x 11" sheets of paper

- Art supplies (markers, pencils, crayons, etc.)

How to Play

Put the big paper in a location that everyone in the group will easily be able to reach. Each group member gets a few minutes to draw part of the picture. When one group member is drawing, other people should wait their turn, not jump in and draw or tell them to draw something else. Don't forget to add something as the group leader - you're a part of the group too! Keep going until each member has had a turn. If the drawing still doesn't seem complete, give everyone one more turn.

Other Ways to Play

- If drawing open-ended is too complex, give the group a theme or a phrase that their drawing has to relate to. You can also start by drawing a line or a squiggle to get their creative juices flowing.

- Take one 8.5 x 11" piece of paper for each group member and lay it in a row, so they're all connected. Make a line that connects all of the pieces of paper. Each group member is assigned one particular piece of paper. Each group member draws on their particular paper. Limit the supplies, so they have to practice waiting their turn for a particular color. When everyone is done, connect all the papers again and see what you created as a group.

- Instead of a drawing, you could do a collage, each person cutting out their own images or words, and taking turns adding it to a group collage.

Debrief Questions

- What was it like to wait your turn and watch other people put in their parts of the drawing?

- Was there ever a time you wished you could speak up and give someone directions or tell them to draw something different?

- What was it like when it was your turn to draw?

- What do you think of your group art creation?

Balloon Tennis

This is a simple way for kids to practice taking turns and get a little movement in as well! If you want to add a little arts and crafts fun to this project, have everyone personalize their racket. Have the group decorate the paper plates and popsicle sticks before you start your balloon tennis game.

Materials Needed

- Paper plates

- Big popsicle sticks

- Balloons

How to Play

Attach one popsicle stick to one paper plate. Make enough so that each child has one "racket." Then blow up balloons for the group to use as balls.

Divide the group into pairs of two. Have partners stand facing each other and give them a balloon to hit back and forth. See how many times they can hit the balloon before it touches the ground. Partners start close together as they get the hang of hitting the balloon. After a few minutes, have each pair take a step back away from one another and see if they can continue to hit the balloon back and forth. After a few more minutes, have them take one more big step back away from each other. Then switch to play pairs tennis, two people on one side, two people on the other with one ball.

Other Ways to Play

- Instead of dividing into pairs, stand in a circle and play as an entire group starting with one balloon (very similar to how you'd play Keep the Ball Up).

- Add in another balloon, and see if the group can keep two balloons going at the same time.

- When you hit the balloon, call out the name of the person you're passing it to. If the person you called doesn't get it, you have to start over.

- Choose an order for the group to touch the balloon and see how many times they can do it without touching the ground. Want a tough challenge? Switch up where members of the group are standing and try it again. Want an even tougher challenge? Add in another balloon!

Debrief Questions

- What were the challenges of taking turns when you were playing with one partner?

- How did that change when you played doubles?

- What did you think of playing tennis with balloons?

Mirror Mirror

This is a game that involves not only taking turns but also paying attention, following the lead of someone else, and it gives group members a chance to be a little silly too!

Materials Needed

Creative ideas for movement

How to Play

The goal of this activity is to have group members take turns mirroring each other's movements. Divide group into pairs. Have the pair figure out who will go first. The person who goes first starts to do a movement (stretching their hand in the air) and their partner mirrors their movements. This continues for a few minutes and may get super silly. After a few minutes, the pairs switch roles. The other person gets a chance to be in charge and choose the movements, while their partner follows their lead.

Other Ways to Play

This game can be played as a whole group. Have all the group members line up facing the person whose movements they will mirror. Everyone mirrors the first person's movements. Then members of the group take turns being the person in charge of the movement.

Debrief Questions

- What was challenging about being the person controlling the movements? What was easy?

- What was challenging about being the mirror? What was easy?

- Which activity did you prefer, mirroring another person's movements, or being the one controlling the movements?

CHAPTER 7

Communication

Communication is the key to human interactions and relationships. Communicating with another person face to face involves both verbal and non-verbal communication. When discussing verbal communication, a great place to start is to help kids get well-versed in how to have a conversation, which involves listening, waiting for your turn to speak and responding to someone else's comments or questions. Here are some basic pointers to share with your group about conversations:

- It's like a tennis game - back and forth with questions and/or comments.

- If you get stuck, ask a follow-up question (Who? What? When? Where? Why? How?).

- Topic changes are allowed and expected in conversations, but if it happens abruptly, it feels awkward. Wait for a break in the conversation. Use phrases like "That reminds me of" or "that makes me think of…"

Remind kids that the tone of voice a person uses and the emphasis of different words can change the meaning of the words. Paying attention to these subtle but important nuances is important to do when discussing communication.

Non-verbal communication, like facial expressions and body language, is another important piece of communication kids need to learn. A lot of communication is done through non-verbals.

As children grow up in the world we live in now, they tend to learn more about communicating in texts or via quick images or videos. While I think it's necessary that kids know how to communicate in this way, it's just as important that they can communicate well when talking face to face with other people. Kids need to be able to communicate effectively both online and in real life. The activities in this chapter focus on real-life interactions, to encourage kids to understand both the verbal and non-verbal aspects of in-person communication.

Quick Tips for Conversations

Good conversations have a back and forth of questions and/or comments.

If you get stuck, ask a follow-up question.

WHO?   WHAT?   WHY?   HOW?
WHEN?   WHERE?

Topic changes are allowed and expected in conversations, but if it happens abruptly, it can feel awkward. If you want to change the topic, wait for a break in the conversation.

**Use phrases like:
that reminds me...
that makes me think of...**

Introductory Discussion Questions

- People communicate with each other in so many ways. Name as many ways as you can think of how people communicate (for example e-mail, texting, phone calls, in-person conversations, FaceTime®, etc).

- Can you give examples of how people communicate without words?

- How do you communicate with your family? How about with your friends?

- Which do you think is the easiest way to communicate?

- Have you ever experienced a miscommunication with someone? What happened?

- Have you ever seen someone saying one thing but their body is saying something else (like they say they're happy, but their shoulder are slumped down, and they are frowning)?

Question Box

A great way for kids to practice communicating with one another is to use a question box. Kids get to practice not only making up questions to start a conversation but answering questions, keeping on topic and staying in a conversation.

Materials Needed

- Small cardboard or wooden box

- Slips of paper

- Pencils

How to Play

First, remind group members of the basics of a good conversation.

Give everyone one slip of paper. Have them write one question on their slip of paper, fold it up and put it in the box.

When everyone has put in their slips of paper, choose one and have the group discuss it. Continue until all the questions are done.

Other Ways to Play

- Give the group a theme or a specific focus for their questions to help them figure out what questions they could write down (for example questions focused on summer, or questions about food or questions about families).

- If you think your group will struggle with creating their own questions, make questions up and have the question box ready to go before group.

Debrief Questions

- Was it hard or easy to come up with a question to add to the box?

- How do you think the conversation went? Did we use good conversational skills as a group?

- Which was your favorite question?

- Are there any other questions you wish we could talk about later?

Interview

Sometimes it helps to have more structure around practice talking back and forth. Use the interview questions as a starting point for practicing asking a question and then asking a follow-up.

Materials Needed

Interview Questions (pg 88)

How to Play

- Cut the Interview Questions printable in half.

- Divide the group into pairs and give each group member in the pair a set of interview questions.

- The group member who has Set 1 of the interview questions begins – they are the interviewer. They ask the other group member (the interviewee) the first question.

- The interviewee listens and responds.

- Once the interviewee has finished answering the question, then they can ask the interviewer, "what about you?" or "what's your answer?"

- Then the group members switch roles.

Other Ways to Play

- Have kids make up their own interview questions, then interview each other.

- Have the group come up with questions together, then break out into pairs and interview each other.

Debrief Questions

- Did you prefer asking the questions or responding to the questions?

- Did you learn anything new about your partner?

- Which was your favorite question? Least favorite?

Interview Questions - Set 1

1. What superhero power would you want and why?

2. If you could design a video game, what would it be like?

3. What is your least favorite part of school?

4. What is your favorite thing to do for fun?

5. What is something that makes you laugh?

Interview Questions - Set 2

1. What is your favorite dessert?

2. If you were a grown-up, what would you forbid?

3. What's the grossest thing that has ever happened to you?

4. Is there a pet you'd like to have?

5. If you had a time machine, when and where would you go?

People Bingo

This is a twist on a traditional bingo game. To cross off a square, you need to find someone who fits the description in the box. How else do you find out about them? Ask them! This is the perfect opportunity to practice asking questions and communicating with one another.

Materials Needed

- People Bingo handout (pg 90)

- Marker or pencil to mark off spots

How to Play

- Give every person in the group a bingo board.

- Once everyone has a board, have kids start to ask each other questions to find someone who fits that description. For example, "are you the youngest person in your family?"

- If they fit the description, then have them initial that square or write their name on the square, and then cross off the box. Keep going until everyone has 5 in a row completed.

Other Ways to Play

Play for a set amount of time instead of playing until everyone has completed 5 in a row.

Debrief Questions

- How did you find people who fit the squares? Was it easy or challenging?

- Were certain squares easier than others?

- Did you learn anything new about group members?

People Bingo

Youngest in the family	Favorite color is blue	Likes to draw	Plays a musical instrument	Can whistle
Has a pet	Has been to a different state	Can rollerskate	Can roll their tongue	Can climb a tree
Has brown eyes	Has a brother or a sister	FREE SPOT	Has played Minecraft®	Plays board games
Favorite season is summer	Has a birthday in the fall	Likes Star Wars®	Likes Chocolate	Plays with LEGO Bricks
Has lived in another state or country	Likes to knit	Loves science	Has broken a bone or needed stitches	Likes reading books

Communicate Without Speaking

You can communicate so much without saying a word. Here's a fun way to practice working on picking up non-verbal signals.

Materials Needed

- Communicate Without Speaking (pg 92)

How to Play

- Print and cut out the printable sheet. Fold each piece and put in a box or container.

- Have kids take turns picking out a scenario to demonstrate. The only rule is, they can't talk at all!

- The rest of the group tries to make smart guesses about what the person is pretending to do. Once they figure it out, it's time for the next person to go.

Other Ways to Play

If it's too much to have group members do it by themselves, have kids work together.

Debrief Questions

- Which one was the easiest to figure out?

- Which one was the hardest?

- What non-verbal cues did you use to figure out what the person was doing?

Reading a book	**Cooking**
Getting ready for bed	**Doing crossword**
Playing a sport (golf, tennis, frisbee, soccer, etc.)	**Walking a dog**
Playing a game (card game, board game, video game)	**Building** (with blocks, LEGO bricks, K'NEX, etc.)

Change the Emphasis, Change the Meaning

The meaning of a sentence can change dramatically based on what feeling you use when you say the words. The meaning can also change depending on which words you emphasize in the sentence. Sometimes, kids don't even realize they are changing the meaning of the sentence by saying things in a certain way.

Materials Needed

- Tone of Voice (pg 95)

How to Play

- Demonstrate how changing the emphasis of one word can change the meaning of the sentence. Try it with this sentence: "I can't wait to go to school today." Say the sentence out loud emphasizing the word "I." Next, try emphasizing "school." And "today." Ask the group members how the emphasis changes the meaning of the sentence. Now have the group members try the activity with the sentence printables. Cut them out and place in a basket, box, or hat. One member picks out a sentence and picks one word to emphasize.

  - The group discusses what the sentence means with that particular word emphasized.

  - Then that same group member reads the sentence with another word emphasized. How does that change the meaning of the sentence?

- Have a different group member pick out another sentence and start again. Keep going until all the sentences are done!

Other Ways to Play

- Instead of emphasizing words, try reading the sentences with different emotions. Say them like you are excited, nervous, mad, happy, etc.

- Use examples from real life - if there's a word or phrase that an adult says, try changing the emphasis or using different emotions and see how that impacts the meaning.

Debrief Questions

- Have you ever noticed when emphasizing words changes the meaning of a sentence at home or during school?

- Or have you seen it in a movie or TV show?

- Can you think of any other sentences that could work for this activity?

- Which one was your favorite sentence?

Ice cream is my favorite.	I'm going to P.E. class.
Let me drive the bus.	When can I go outside?
It's time to go.	Did you see that?
You are the best sister ever.	This is some trip.
I love swimming.	Let's play Monopoly®.

CHAPTER 8
Personal Space

There are lots of different ways people describe personal space. Kids may have heard personal space described as a hula hoop, or your space bubble, or making sure you keep an arm's length away from someone.

Personal space is a challenging concept for kids, because how comfortable you feel with someone changes depending on your relationship. When you feel very comfortable and safe with someone (like members of your family or your best friend), you will feel more comfortable being physically close to them. But if you've just met someone for the first time, you will feel less comfortable being physically close to them.

Personal space can also change depending on where you are. If you're on a crowded public transportation bus or leaving a huge event, you're obviously going to get physically closer to strangers than you typically would.

Your comfort level with personal space can also change depending on your moods or emotions. Sometimes, when people are upset, they wish to be left alone, and don't want to be touched or hugged. Others want hugs or physical comfort when they're upset.

People can use their communication skills to help manage their personal space.

For example, when someone is getting too close:

"You're getting too close."

"Can you please back up?"

"I need a little space."

Or when someone is too far away:

"You can come closer."

"You're too far away."

Introductory Discussion Questions

- What sorts of words or phrases have you heard to describe personal space?

- How does personal space differ between your family and someone you don't know at all?

- How do your feelings impact personal space?

- What can you say if you want someone to give you more personal space?

- What can you say if you want someone to come a little closer?

Make an Obstacle Course

Work together as a group, use your imagination and create an obstacle course. You can do an obstacle course indoors, or you can set one up outdoors. Encourage group members to pay attention to their personal space as they go through the obstacle course.

Materials Needed

These are just some ideas; you can use whatever you have on hand, indoors or out, to create an obstacle course:

- Jump rope
- Plastic cones
- Blocks
- Cups
- Chairs
- Gym mat
- Scooter

How to Play

Work together to set up the course. Once you set it up, time the group to see how fast they can get through it. Then try a different setup and see how well you get through that one.

Other Ways to Play

Give each group member a chance to create an obstacle course for the group to complete.

Debrief Questions

- How did you have to keep personal space in mind when you were going through this activity?
- How would this activity have gone differently if you did it with your family?
- How about with someone you'd never met before?

Rabbit Hole Game

This is a game of tag with a twist!

Materials Needed

- 3 hula hoops
- Several cones

How to Play

Before group

Place the hula hoops in different parts of the room. Balance them on top of the cones, so the hula hoops are a few inches off of the ground.

To begin

Designate one group member to be a fox, and the rest of the group members are pretending to be rabbits. The fox chases the rabbits and tries to tag them. The hula hoops are the rabbit holes. When a rabbit is in the hole, they are safe. If a rabbit gets tagged, then they become a fox, and start to chase the remaining rabbits.

Optional Rule: If a hoop is knocked off the cones, all the rabbits in that hole become foxes!

- Start the game with three hoops.
- Once that round is over, choose another fox and play again with just two hoops.
- After that round, choose a different fox and play one more time with just one hoop.

Other Ways to Play

- Place the hula hoops on the ground instead of balancing them on cones.
- Use a rope or string to make bigger rabbit holes. Or use both rope and hula hoops to make different sized rabbit holes.

Debrief Questions

- Did you prefer being a fox or a rabbit?
- When did you have to think about personal space when you were playing the first round? The second? The third?
- Would you have felt comfortable being in the rabbit hole with someone you didn't know? How about with a member of your family?

Newspaper Dancing

Sometimes it helps to have a visual when you're thinking about different levels of comfort when it comes to personal space. This lesson is not only fun but demonstrates how personal space changes.

Materials Needed

- Newspaper
- Music

How to Play

Give every group member their own big piece of newspaper and put them all in a circle on the floor. Tell the group members that when a song comes on, their job is to dance. The only rule is they have to stay on their own newspaper piece when they dance. Put on a song and have fun!

Then, pause the music and have them fold their newspaper piece in half. Bring the circle in closer, since the newspaper pieces are smaller. Remind the kids about the rule to stay on their own spot, and begin dancing.

Once more, stop the music and have kids fold their paper once more. Bring the pieces in closer to one another and put on a song.

Other Ways to Play

- Use different layers of fabric circle to convey the different levels of personal space, for example:

    - A small green circle/square to represent the child
    - People who are family - slightly bigger yellow circle/square
    - People who are friends - slightly bigger orange circle/square
    - People who are strangers - big purple circle/square

Debrief Questions

- How easy was it to keep your own personal space when your newspaper piece was big?

- How did it change after you folded it the first time?

- And how did it change after you folded it the second time?

Walk and Stop

Kids should know their boundaries. This is a quick activity to help kids get a better understanding of not only their own boundaries but also the boundaries of other kids as well.

Materials Needed

- A space big enough for kids to walk towards each other

- A measuring tape or big ruler

- Paper to write down measurements

How to Play

Have the group break out into pairs.

The first person walks towards the second person in the pair. When the second person feels like their partner is close enough, they raise their hand and say stop.

Measure the distance between the two people, and write down the measurement.

Keep going until everyone has done the activity with everyone else in the group.

Other Ways to Play

You can just do the activity without writing down the measurements.

Debrief Questions

- Do you notice any patterns in the measurements?

- What factors influence how close you let someone get to you?

- What would have happened if you did this activity with a member of your family? Your teacher? Someone you just met?

Hip Ball Race

This is an activity that requires people to be comfortable with getting close to each other and working together.

Materials Needed

- Several balls of different sizes
- Start and finish line

How to Play

Divide the group up into pairs. Have each pair choose a ball. The pair stands next to each other and puts the ball in between their bodies. They should get close enough together that their bodies push on either side of the ball and the ball is stable between them. Once everyone is ready, have them line up at the start line. Let the race begin! Keeping the balls in place, see which pair crosses the finish line first. Once the first race is over, either switch up pairs or switch balls (or both) and have the group race again.

Other Ways to Play

- Want a challenge? Try three people walking side by side with two balls in between!
- Want an incredible challenge? Have your entire group do it together!

Debrief Questions

- How close did you have to get to make this activity work?
- How was the first race different from the second?
- What was easy about this activity? What was challenging?

CHAPTER 9

Being Kind

Practicing being kind and showing compassion for other people is important. Remember the old saying, "You catch more flies with honey than with vinegar"? It's a good reminder that approaching people in a kind, compassionate manner can have a positive outcome on social interactions. When you have a choice, choose kind.

Kindness is part of what it means to be a good friend. To be a good and kind friend, you need to think about the other person's needs and wants. You can't always have it your way, or be the one in charge all the time. You have to think about what your friend would like. It's challenging, and it takes practice to think about someone else and make a decision based on what they would like. Being kind is a skill that can be practiced and nurtured.

One huge thing you as the group leader can do is model kind behavior. Our students are watching how we talk and interact not only with them but also with other adults. You want your students to be able to see good examples of kindness, and watching how you interact with others is a teachable moment for them!

Introductory Discussion Questions

- What does it mean to be kind?

- When was the last time you saw someone do something kind?

- Has anyone ever done something kind for you? Share what happened.

- How can you show kindness at school? At home?

- Have you ever heard of a random act of kindness? Have you ever done a random act of kindness?

Kindness Wall

Here's a great way to publicly recognize the kind acts that kids do!

Materials Needed

Kindness Means & Stars (pgs 107-108)

How to Play

Talk as a group about what kindness means. As kids generate ideas, either have them write the idea on the "kindness means…" page, or write it on there yourself. Explain that you will be starting a kindness wall, where you recognize a kind act that someone has done, and you're starting today.

Give every person a star, and have them think about a person who has done a kind act recently. The group member writes down the kind person's name and what they did. Once everyone has filled in a star, then find a spot to start your kindness wall. Place the filled out "kindness means" printable on the wall, and put the stars around it. Anytime kids are caught being kind, their name and kind deed is added to a star, then place it on the wall! You can also use the stars to recognize kind acts that you do as a group if you complete other activities in this chapter.

Other Ways to Play

- Instead of using stars, use thin strips of paper and create a chain to hang around the kindness means poster.

- Instead of stars, use people-shaped cutouts, and place the cutouts on the wall so that they are all connected.

Debrief Questions

- How did it feel to recognize other people for their kindness?

- Have you ever been recognized for doing something kind? What was that like?

- If you were to do a kind act for someone, what would it be?

- What sort of kindness activities could we do as a group?

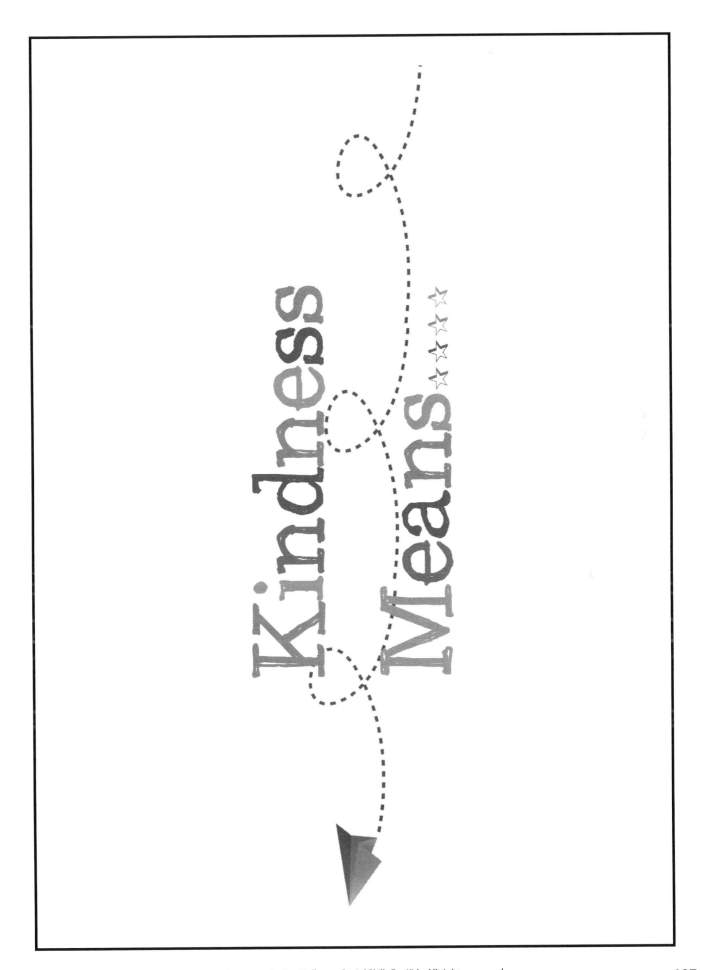

Kindness Means

Make a Puzzle and Give It Away

This activity combines creativity and kindness. Kids make a puzzle then pick a person to give the puzzle to as an act of kindness.

Materials Needed

- Blank puzzles (available online)

- Crayons

- Small labels with the names of the group members placed in a hat

- Plastic bags

How to Play

Each person in the group gets one puzzle to decorate. Here's the kind part - the puzzle is for another member of the group! Have each child pick a label out of the hat and keep it face down (they just can't pick themselves!). Once everyone knows who they are making a puzzle for, let the imagination and creativity begin!

When everyone is done making a puzzle, put each puzzle into a plastic bag and put the name label on it. Then have the group exchange, and give the puzzles to their new owners.

Other Ways to Play

- Instead of making puzzles for one another in secret, keep all the labels face up. This way, you can ask the person you are making it for what they like, what they enjoy or what their favorite colors are. Then the group members draw pictures or patterns based on what they said.

- Everyone makes a puzzle, then puzzles can get randomly exchanged at the end.

Debrief Questions

- What did you think of this activity?

- How did you feel when you finished the puzzle and gave it away?

- How did the other person feel when they got it?

- Was it hard to keep it a secret from the person was going to get the puzzle?

Thank You!

With the previous puzzle activity, the group did something kind for each other. With this activity, the group is going to do something kind for people outside of the group.

Materials Needed

- Blank cards

- Crayons, markers, colored pencils

How to Play

Talk as a group about people in your life who do something for you, but don't always get thanked. Make a list of those people and talk through examples of things they've done for you. Here are some ideas of people you could write a thank you note to:

- The bus driver

- Your teacher

- The school secretary

- The UPS® delivery person

- The mail carrier

- A member of your family (like your mom, dad, grandmother, grandfather, aunt, uncle, cousin, etc.)

Each group member identifies a person they want to thank, and specific reasons why they want to thank them. These reasons can be used as inspiration for the cards. Then get started!

After the group is over, deliver your card and watch how surprised and happy they are to receive such a thoughtful gift from you!

Other Ways to Play

Narrow down the categories of people who kids can make cards for - for example, the focus could be a person in the school, so that could be their OT, or the custodian, or the librarian. Or if the focus is a family member, it could be an aunt, a cousin, or a grandpa.

Debrief Questions

- Who did you pick and why?

- How do you think they will react when they get this card?

- If you want, at the beginning of the next group, ask group members to share how their card recipients reacted once they received their special surprises.

Acts of Kindness

Doing something unexpected and kind for someone who has no idea is an amazing activity. You can perform an act of kindness for someone you know, or for someone you don't. What a great group activity!

How to Play

Choose one of the following acts of kindness.

- Decorate notes or stones with inspirational messages or rainbows and leave it in unexpected places for people to find (in a garden, at a dog park, on someone's desk).

- Collect socks and other supplies and donate to a homeless shelter.

- Collect canned goods and donate to a local food shelter.

- Hand out stickers to other kids at school.

- Donate books to a local doctor's office waiting room.

- Make bookmarks and donate to the library.

- Arrange to read books to a class of younger students.

- Set up a local park/playground clean-up day.

- Donate games and toys to a local children's hospital.

- Make playdough and give it away.

Other Ways to Play

Don't see an act of kindness that works for your group? Make up your own!

Debrief Questions

- How did it feel when you were gathering all the materials needed?

- How did you feel when you finished the act of kindness?

- Did you get a chance to see how people reacted to your act of kindness?

- If you didn't, how do you think they reacted?

The Domino Effect - Pay It Forward

Doing kind acts for others often encourages them to do their own kind acts. Demonstrate the impact that kind acts have by using Dominoes.

Materials Needed: Dominoes

How to Play

Discuss how kind acts can lead to other kind acts. For example, if someone holds a door open, then that person often feels happier, and it's more likely that they'll do another kind act for someone else, and so forth.

First, set up only two dominoes in a row. Then knock the first one into the second one. Discuss with the group that these two Dominoes knocking together doesn't make a huge impact. Then ask the group to guess what would happen if you added more dominoes.

Ask kids to talk about kind acts that they've seen or done. As each child mentions a kind act, either have them place a Domino in a row or place the domino yourself. When you've gotten at least 20 kind acts, then knock it down again. How much more of an impact did that make!

Other Ways to Play

- Instead of using dominoes, you can demonstrate the multiplying effect of kindness using a piece of paper. Before you begin, ask kids how many corners the paper has. As kids mention kind acts, cut off a corner of the paper. Once they've mentioned several kind acts, ask them to count the corners again.

- To discuss the ripple effect of kind acts, use a deep pan, filled halfway with water, and a penny for every person in the group. Have everyone in the group take turns dropping their penny into the water. Explain that the penny represents kind acts and point out the ripple effect that multiple kind acts has on the water.

Debrief Questions

- What was the effect of knocking down Dominoes when there were only two on the table?

- How did that change when we had 20 on the table?

- Have you ever noticed when someone did a kind act after someone did a kind act for them?

CHAPTER 10
Feelings Identification

There are so many types of social skills that we as humans use on a daily basis. So far, we've discussed outward skills - social skills that involve interacting with other people. But there's a whole other set of social skills that involves a person's inner world. We need to have an understanding of our thoughts and feelings. Once we have a better understanding of ourselves, we can interact with others more easily.

Feelings identification is an essential skill for kids. It's good to start practicing identifying those different feelings early on in life. Identifying feelings is a great first step in helping kids learn to manage those emotions. Some kids have an easier time being able to identify their feelings, others struggle. These activities will help your group get familiar with emotion words and start to make connections between their thoughts, their behaviors, the things that are happening around them and how they feel.

Introductory Discussion Questions

- What makes kids feel happy?

- What makes kids feel sad?

- What makes kids feel worried?

- What makes kids feel angry?

- How do kids show their different feelings?

- What makes it easier to figure out how you are feeling?

- What makes it harder to figure out how you are feeling?

- Sometimes people have more than one feeling at a time. Have you ever seen that happen or had that happen yourself?

Make Your Own Feeling Faces Chart

Feelings Faces Charts can help kids identify what they are feeling, or help them figure out what others might have been feeling. This activity gives your group an opportunity to make a fun visual together that can help them identify emotions. Plus it sets up a teachable moment to have conversations about what happens to somebody's face when they feel certain ways.

Materials Needed

- Magazines/newspapers/photos of children's faces
- Poster board

How to Play

Start by identifying a few feelings you want on your chart. You could keep it as simple as happy, mad, sad, and scared. Or you could make it a little bit more complex and add in feelings like embarrassed, worried, frustrated, silly or confused.

Working as a group, gather images of real kids showing different emotions from magazines or newspaper flyers or on stock photo sites like pixabay.com. Talk about how people's faces look when they feel certain ways, for example:

- When a person is mad, a person's eyebrows are pulled down, and their lips may be tight.

- When a person is scared, their eyebrows are pulled up and together, and their mouth is stretched.

- When a person is happy, their cheeks are raised, and their lip corners are raised diagonally.

- When they are sad, the inner corner of their eyes are raised, their eyelids are loose, and the corners of their mouth are pulled down.

Cut out the pictures or print out photos and write the feeling each face represents underneath the photos.

Once it's all done, post it someplace that can be easily accessed. Next time you want to use a feelings face chart, you can now use this personalized kid friendly chart.

Other Ways to Play

- You can put more than one face for each emotion.

- You can use your own students' images, as long as you have permission to photograph them. Have kids make different feelings faces, and make a genuinely personalized group feelings faces chart.

- Instead of using real faces, you could also use emojis.

Debrief Questions

- Which feelings were easy to find and identify?

- Which feelings were more challenging to find?

- Are there any other emotions you think we should put on our chart?

Mixed Up Emotions

This is perfect for having a little fun while learning about how eyes and mouths look when people feel certain ways.

Materials Needed

- Mixed Up Emotions (pg 119)

- Paper plates

- Yarn

- Markers/crayons/colored pencils

- Ribbons or yarn

How to Play

Cut out all the eyes and the mouths. Have the group members make combinations of eyes and mouths and try to figure out what feeling they created with their combination. Sometimes combinations work, and sometimes they don't. Make silly combinations and try to figure out what feeling the face is showing.

Once you've had some fun combining mouths and eyes, have each group member pick one set of eyes and one mouth and take a paper plate. Now they can create their own crazy face. They can add hair using the yarn or ribbon, or draw in other features. This is an opportunity for kids to get as creative as they want!

Other Ways to Play

Try to make the eyes and mouths match a specific feeling.

Debrief Questions

- Which was the silliest combination of eyes and mouth we made? What feeling did it look like?

- What made you choose the eyes and mouth you did?

- Share your silly face creation with the group!

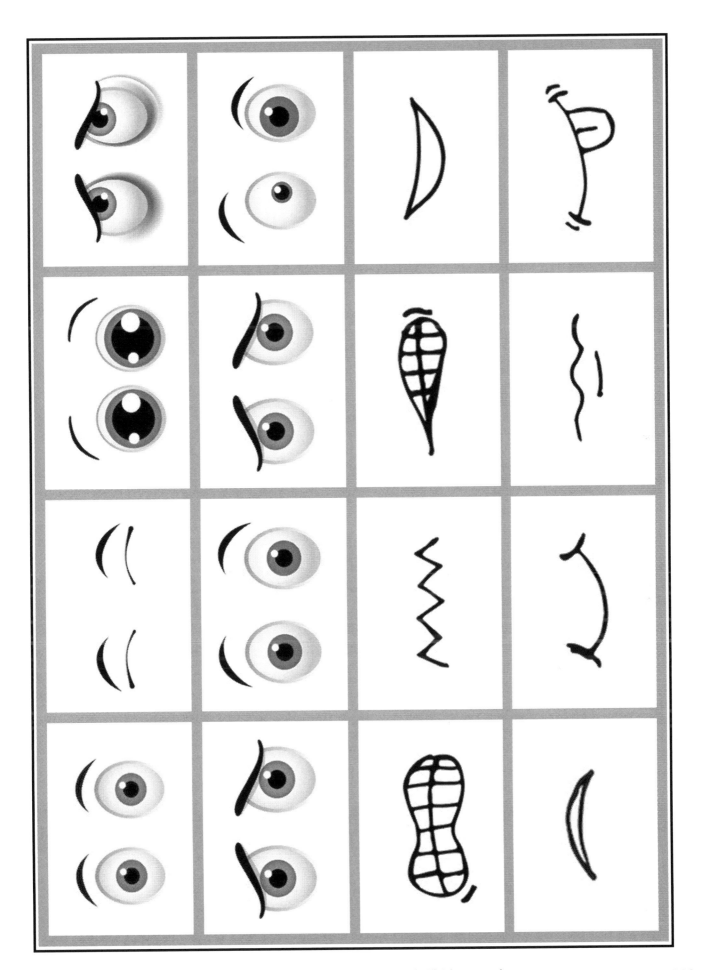

Chain of Feelings

Use paper chains as a visual to show how people in your group feel about different situations. This is a neat visual and can give you useful information as you are working together. For instance, you may discover that everyone in your group has a hard time before school or at bedtime.

Materials Needed

- Chain of Feelings (pg 122)

- Tape

- Construction paper of four different colors, cut into long strips.
    - Red = frustrated/angry

    - Green = calm/happy/good

    - Blue = sad/tired

    - Yellow = worried/scared

How to Play

Cut out the places/experiences printable and place each one on the walls in the room with a good amount of space between them. Place one circle of construction paper on the wall, below the printable to serve as the start of a paper chain.

Put the different colors of construction paper in different piles.

Explain that there are several places/scenarios that the group members experience during a regular week, and you're going to do an activity that will show how everyone in the group feels about those activities.

Tell the group members which feelings match which colors of construction paper. Then show the group how to make a chain using the construction paper strip and tape. Send one group member to one paper posted on the wall. Ask them to think about which category of feelings they usually have during that activity, then pick a corresponding color, write their name on it and make a paper chain. They add their link to that chain; then they move on to the next scenario.

For instance, in math, if they usually feel calm, have them get a green piece of construction paper, write their name on it, and add it to the chain below math. Then they move on to the next one. Keep going until everyone has put a link at every scenario.

Other Ways to Play

- Want to discuss other feelings? Add more colors!

- Want to explore other typical experiences or scenarios that happen to your group members? Put those in too!

Debrief Questions

- What patterns did you notice in our chains?

- What color would your family's chains be for any of these scenarios at home? Would it match yours or would it be different?

- What color would your teacher's link be? Would it match yours or would it be different?

- What do we as a group have in common?

At Bedtime	After School
Recess	Math
Reading	Lunch
Free Time	Before School

Beanbag Feelings Game

This activity helps kids identify how certain situations might make them feel. It also helps kids recognize that different kids may feel different ways about the same situation.

Materials Needed

- Beanbags (at least two for each person in the group)

- Feelings (pg 125)

- Space on the floor or outside

How to Play

- Cut out the feelings and tape them to a floor or rug.

- Give examples of situations that kids may experience. Then have the group members throw their beanbag on the feeling or feelings that they would have in that situation.

Here are some examples to get you started:

- You just got 3rd place in the spelling bee. How would you feel?

- You got an A on a test. How would you feel?

- Your friend stopped talking to you. How would you feel?

- You just found out there's no school today. How would you feel?

- Your grandma is coming for a visit. How would you feel?

- You have a playdate tomorrow. How would you feel?

- Tonight is movie night, and your sister is picking the movie. How would you feel?

Other Ways to Play

If you don't have beanbags, spread the feeling printables out over a bigger area, and have kids move their bodies to the feeling or feelings they might feel in that particular situation.

Debrief Questions

- Was it hard to figure out what you would feel in those situations?

- Did you ever feel like there was more than one feeling you'd have in a situation? What did you do?

- Have you ever had a hard time figuring out how you were feeling in a situation?

Happy	Sad
Angry	Stressed
Scared	Anxious

Emotion Animal Charades

This is a fun way to practice demonstrating different feelings and pretending to be different animals. This is sure to lead to lots of silliness and laughter.

Materials Needed

- Animal Cards (pg 127)
- Emotion Cards (pg 128)

How to Play

Cut out all of the emotion and animal cards. Put them in two piles on the table. Each person in the group gets an opportunity to perform an animal charade. They pick an emotion and an animal and act it out. The rest of the group has to figure out what the emotion and the animal are.

Some possible combinations include:

- Scared bunny
- Sleepy turtle
- Sad cat

Keep going until all the animals and emotions have been used.

Other Ways to Play

If one group member is feeling unsure, or unwilling to do it alone, have two go together at the same time, performing the same emotion animal charade. Or have one group member show the feeling while the other shows the animal.

Debrief Questions

- Which combination was the easiest for you to figure out?
- Which combination was the hardest?
- How was it acting out your animal charade?
- Which did you prefer, acting or guessing?

Scared	Happy
Silly	Sleepy
Sneaky	Mad
Sad	Surprised

CHAPTER 11
Coping with Feelings

As was mentioned in the previous chapter, some social skills don't involve only interacting with other people, and but also our ability to manage ourselves. We covered understanding feelings in the last chapter. Another vital skill to for children to practice is the ability to cope with those feelings in safe and healthy ways.

Sometimes it seems like kids think that they shouldn't ever get mad, or frustrated, or sad. It's normal that we will feel a range of emotions during our lives, even during a day. And it's expected to feel big feelings, but it's how you deal with those feelings that matter. The explanation I use with my clients is that it's okay to feel anything, as long as you:

- don't hurt yourself

- don't hurt others

- don't hurt property

Kids can learn to identify and manage their feelings using coping skills.

Introductory Discussion Questions

- Which feelings are easy to manage?

- Which feelings are harder to manage?

- How do kids deal with big feelings?

- How do you cope with feeling sad? Angry? Worried?

Deep Breathing Die

Deep breathing is one of the first steps I take in teaching kids to calm down and relax. Let me explain why deep breathing is so important.

When you are calm, your body is in what is known as "rest and digest" mode. Your breathing is normal, your muscles are relaxed, and your heart rate is normal.

When you experience a stressful event, your body automatically goes into what is known as "flight, fight or freeze" mode. Your heart rate increases, your stomach stops digestion, and your breathing becomes more shallow.

Deep breathing tells your body that it is time to switch from "flight, fight or freeze" mode back to "rest and digest" mode. Deep breathing helps get more oxygen into your bloodstream, opening up your capillaries. It has a physical effect on your body to help you calm down and lower stress.

This is a playful way to try several different deep breathing strategies.

Materials Needed

- Deep Breathing Die (pg 132) - one for each person in the group - for a sturdier cube, print on cardstock

- Scissors

- Scotch tape

How to Play

Before group:

Put one die together to use as a template

During group:

- Have each group member take a turn rolling your die. When the die lands, the whole group practices the deep breathing idea on the side facing up.

- Once everyone has had a turn, then it's time for the group members to make their own dice to take home.

- Give each group member a deep breathing die sheet (if you want a sturdier cube, print on cardstock).

- Have each group member cut out a die, and fold along the lines.

- Gently fold the paper into a cube. Tuck in the flaps and tape all the sides down.

- Encourage group members to play at home with their families!

Other Ways to Play

Other props to use to encourage deep breathing:

- Bubbles

- Pinwheels

- Hoberman Sphere®

- Feathers

Use videos to demonstrate and practice deep breathing:

- Watch the GoZen video of 4-7-8 Breathing

- Watch the Coping Skills for Kids video of Deep Breathing with Shapes

- Watch the GoNoodle video of Rainbow Breath

Debrief Questions

- Which was your favorite way to take a deep breath?

- Which was your least favorite way?

- Are there other ways you can think of to take deep breaths?

Deep Breathing Die

Smell the soup, cool down the soup

Take a deep breath in, and pretend to blow a bubble

Breathe in blue skies, breathe out gray skies

Breathe in for 4 counts, breathe out for 5 counts

Raise your arms & breathe in, lower your arms & breathe out

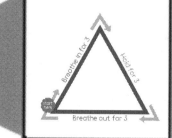

DIY Calming Jar

Making calming jars with kids is fun, but it's also a useful coping strategy that can help a child calm down and relax. Calming jars can be used as a way to take space when things get a little overwhelming. Just shake the jar and watch the glitter settle to the bottom. There is something very calming about shaking the bottle and watching the glitter or other materials slowly settle down. At our house, we use them at bedtime and as a way to relax.

Materials Needed

- Empty water bottle - enough for every person in the group

- Warm water

- Glitter paint

How to Play

To make your jar, add glitter paint to the bottom of the jar until it just covers the bottom of it. Add warm water. Put the cover on and shake to help the ingredients combine.

Once you are satisfied with the look of your jar, then you can super glue the lid shut, so it doesn't spill. In a pinch, I've also used duct tape to secure the lid.

Now, let's see the calming jar in action.

First, do a quick feelings check in with the whole group.

Then, have every group member shake up their calming jar, and watch it.

Once it's settled, check in about how they are feeling again.

Do they feel the same way?

Other Ways to Play

Here are some other optional ingredients you can use in a calming jar. Using thicker wet ingredients will make the dry ingredients sink slower.

Wet Ingredients

- Hair gel

- Corn syrup

- Glue

133

- Glitter glue

- Glow in the dark paint

Dry Ingredients

- LEGOs

- Glitter

- Small stones

- Small shells

- Glow in the dark stars

Debrief Questions

- Did you notice a difference between how you felt before you used the calming jar and after you used it?

- When do you think it would be beneficial to use your calming jar?

- Are there other things you wish you could add to your jar?

Make Cloud Dough

Kids respond well to sensory play, and this is a great one. This activity uses their sense of smell and touch which can help them relax. The smell depends on what kind of conditioner you use.

Materials Needed

- 2 parts of cornstarch
- 1 part hair conditioner
- Small bowls and spoons for mixing
- Wax paper
- Cookie cutters
- Plastic containers for each child

How to Play

Give each child a bowl, and put 2 parts cornstarch, and one part conditioner in each bowl. Have group members mix their ingredients together to create their cloud dough. Once it's combined and workable, then have kids put the dough on the wax paper and play with it. Encourage kids to use the cookie cutters and play with the dough. When they are done, put their dough in plastic containers to take home.

Other Ways to Play

Instead of cloud dough, you can make no-cook playdough:

- 1 cup cold water
- 1 cup salt
- 2 teaspoons vegetable oil
- 3 cups flour
- 2 tablespoons cornstarch
- Tempera paint or food coloring (optional)

In bowl, mix water, salt, oil, and paint/food coloring (optional). Gradually add flour and cornstarch until the mixture reaches the consistency of bread dough (kneading with hands is a great sensory activity). Store in a plastic bag or covered container.

Debrief Questions

- How did you like making the cloud dough?

- Did you like the scent? If not, what kind of scent would you prefer?

- How did you end up playing with the dough?

- Do you remember how you felt before you started playing with it?

- How did you feel after you were done playing with it?

Mindful Senses

Mindfulness is being aware of what's happening in the present moment. It's not about trying to clear your mind, but allowing thoughts and emotions to come and go without judgment and familiarizing ourselves with the present moment. It takes practice to be able to do this.

Mindfulness can be a helpful tool for kids who have challenges with self-regulation or difficulty managing emotions or want to improve their concentration. This mindful senses activity is a fun way to introduce the concept of mindfulness to kids.

Materials Needed

- Cut flowers

- Small piece of fruit or chocolate (blackberries, Hershey's® kiss, potato chip, pumpkin seeds, etc.)

How to Play

Sight & Smell

Give each group member a flower. Tell them to take a few moments to look at the flower in front of them and see what they notice.

- What colors do they see?

- What patterns do they see?

- What does it smell like?

- As they kept looking, did they notice a detail that they hadn't seen at first?

Taste & Feel

Hand out a snack to every member of the group. Let's use the blackberry as an example.

Before they do anything, have your group members take a moment to look at the blackberry. Notice all the details about the blackberry. How big is it? What color is it? Is it softer or a little bit firmer? How heavy or light does it feel in your hand?

Take a moment and sniff it – does it have a strong scent or a faint scent?

Next, ask group members to put the blackberry in their mouth, but don't chew and swallow it quickly. Notice how the berry feels in your mouth. Chew it several times, paying attention to the sensations and the tastes. What changes as your chew? Once you have chewed it thoroughly and you are ready, swallow the blackberry.

Other Ways to Play

Instead of doing all these during one group, you can use it as a starting activity or an ending activity during group.

(You can also do the Mindful Listening Activity from Chapter 1)

Debrief Questions

- Which was your favorite activity?

- What did you notice during this activity that you never noticed before?

- What other item could you use for the sight & smell activity?

- What other item could use you for the taste & feel activity?

Calm Down Kit

A calm down kit is an actual physical container that houses items kids can use to help calm down and express their emotions in healthy ways. There are a ton of strategies your child can use to calm down, and having a toolbox is one way to keep several of these tools readily available to use. It's important to have a few different coping strategies available in a calm down kit. Not all skills will work all the time, so it's good to have a few to choose from in their kit.

In terms of providing skills for them to choose from, make sure you offer a variety. What works for one person may not work for another one. What works will vary, depending on their feelings, their temperament, their favorite activities and their energy level at that moment.

Materials Needed

- Word search pages
- Crossword puzzles
- Bubbles
- Fidgets - cut up pool noodles, Wikki Stix® and/or small spiky balls
- Bubble wrap
- Paper and pencils
- Container to hold all the calm down strategies
- Label for Calm Down Kit (pg 141)

(This is a suggested list - if there are other items you have on hand, or you want to offer to your group, please feel free to add those in)

How to Play

Lay out all the materials that you've supplied for kids to make their own calm down kit.

Set up stations so that kids can try the different materials. For instance, at the bubbles station, have a bubble container that's already been opened ready for kids to try and see if it helps them with their deep breathing. Have extra word searches printed for kids to try and see if they find it relaxing, etc.

After everyone has tried all the stations, have group members pick out items they want to put in their calm down kit. Have them pick out at least three items.

Once they've figured out what can go in their calm down kit, then have them decorate their label to personalize their own kit.

Other ideas

- Don't forget that some of the activities earlier in this chapter can be part of this calm down kit as well. See if they want to add in their calming jar, their cloud dough or their deep breathing dice printable.

- Remind them that this is their own personal calm down kit and they can add other items to it that they think would help.

Debrief Questions

- When do you think you'll use this calm down kit? Will it work at home, at school, or both?

- How is your kit the same as other members of the group? How is it different?

- What other calming tools could you add to it?

My Calm Down Kit

_____

My Calm Down Kit

_____

My Calm Down Kit

_____

My Calm Down Kit

_____

My Calm Down Kit

_____

My Calm Down Kit

_____

CHAPTER 12

Self-Regulation

Self-regulation is another social skill that involves a person's inner world. So far, we've focused on identifying feelings and coping with them. Self-regulation is related to these but is specifically focused on managing frustration, controlling impulses, and delaying gratification.

The ability to self-regulate is impacted by a child's personality, their temperament, and their history. Certain kids may struggle more with self-regulation. However, just like other skills it can be practiced and learned through play.

One thing that kids who have difficulty controlling their impulses struggle with is not thinking before they speak. There are a couple of ways that may help them become less impulsive with their speech. One thing is to talk about using a filter when you're speaking. It's ok to think any thought you want to think, but not all thoughts are good to say. You can even use a coffee filter as a visual. Another way to visualize it is to use a thought bubble and a talk bubble. Those thoughts that should stay in your head and not get verbalized can be put in thought bubbles, while the thoughts it's ok to say can be put in talk bubbles.

Another statement kids can keep in mind is to think before you speak. Is what you are about to say:

True

Helpful

Inspiring

Necessary

Kind

If not, stop and think before you speak.

Introductory Discussion Questions

- What does self-regulation mean?

- When do you have a hard time waiting?

- What makes it easier to wait for something? Harder?

- Sometimes, kids struggle with not thinking before they speak. Have you ever seen that happen?

- What do you think helps kids think before they speak?

The Pink Panther Game

This is a game that's all about controlling your facial expressions. Try not to smile or laugh!

Materials Needed

Ideas to make other kids laugh or smile

How to Play

All members sit in chairs and put on a serious face.

Pick one group member to be the Pink Panther® - his goal is to get the other students to laugh or smile. He can make faces, tell jokes, dance, or do anything he wants (that's appropriate, of course) except touch them.

Once someone smiles or laughs, they join the Pink Panther in trying to get the other kids to smile. The group member that doesn't crack a smile and is the last person left becomes the next Pink Panther.

Other Ways to Play

You as the group leader can be the Pink Panther first. Or if you want to do something kind of fun, bring in other adults who work with your students to play the Pink Panther.

Debrief Questions

- What was your favorite thing about being the Pink Panther?

- When you were the Pink Panther, what seemed to work the best to make kids smile/laugh?

- When you were a player, what did you do to keep yourself from smiling or laughing? Which strategy worked the best for you?

Night at the Museum

Quick, don't let the night manager catch you! Everyone has to pretend to be statues, and they can't move when the night manager is watching. But who knows what will happen when the night manager isn't watching.

Materials Needed

- Open space

- Flashlight (or something that could be seen as a flashlight)

How to Play

Pick one group member to be the night manager, and the rest of the group will be statues. The night manager moves slowly around the room, looking and watching, and putting his flashlight on the "statues" in the museum. If the flashlight is on you, stay as still as you can. If you move or laugh, you're out for the round. But when the night manager is not watching, you can move! Take turns having group members be the night manager.

Other Ways to Play

When you get caught, instead of being out, you go to a designated area and do five wall push-ups to get back into the game.

Debrief Questions

- Did you prefer being a night manager or a statue?

- Were you able to move around without getting caught? How did you do that?

- How do you think this game relates to self-regulation?

Freeze Dance

A simple way to help kids practice starting and stopping unexpectedly, a great way to practice self-control.

Materials Needed

- Room to dance
- Music - 2 or 3 different tempo or styles of songs

How to Play

Explain to the group that you will be doing a freeze dance. When the music is on, then everyone just has a great time dancing. Then when the music stops, everyone stops! See how group members are able to stop. Then change the song. If the first song you did was fast, then try a slower song. Or try a different style of a song, switching from a pop song to a classical one. Dance and have fun!

Other Ways to Play

Instead of freeze dance, you can play musical chairs.

Debrief Questions

- How did you do with freezing when the song had stopped?
- During which song was it easiest to stop? Why?
- During which song was it hardest to stop? Why?

Relay Races

Kids have to wait their turn to run their part of a relay race. This activity involves movement, paying attention, and waiting for your turn!

Materials Needed

- Start and finish lines
- Long space to run (hallway, recess blacktop area, gymnasium)
- Baton (paper towel tube)
- Timer

How to Play

Explain to kids that they'll be running a race, but instead of all running at the same time, they'll be running one at a time, as part of a team. Each person takes a turn and runs up and back, then hands off the baton to the next person in line. Have kids practice how to hand off the baton. Then, pick the order in which kids will run.

Finally, it's time to race. Start the timer, and have the kids begin their race. Have them encourage one another with positive words to the person running when they're waiting. Keep track of how long it took for them to complete the race. See if they can improve their relay race skills and beat their first time.

Other Ways to Play

- Instead of running, have kids skip, or crab walk, or move in other ways to complete the race.

- Depending on the size of the group, you may want to divide the group in half, putting 3 to 4 kids on one relay team. Have the groups race against each other, using this as an opportunity to discuss good sportsmanship. They can even decorate their team's batons!

Debrief Questions

- What was your experience doing the relay race?
- What did you do while you waited for your turn?
- What were your thoughts and/or feelings during the race? Once it was all over?

DIY Scratch Art

This lesson will be completed in two different group lesson times. During the first lesson, you complete the steps to make your own scratch art paper. Then the next week, the group can use their scratch art paper and make a unique drawing.

Materials Needed

- Card stock
- Crayons
- Black tempera paint
- Toothpick, chopstick or small wooden dowel

How to Play

Week One

- Take the card stock and make a pattern using a black crayon. You can make a grid, or waves, or make big swirls (my favorite way).
- Color in every block using different colors.
- Once the whole picture has been colored in, then cover the paper with black tempera paint. It may take more than one layer to cover it up completely. None of the original colors should be visible. Now it's time to wait!

Week Two

- After it's dry, take a chopstick or toothpick and create a picture by scratching off the layer of tempera paint. Underneath, you'll see the colors you originally created.

Other Ways to Play

Instead of waiting a week and doing the project in group, kids can bring their artwork home and complete their picture there once it's dry.

Debrief Questions

- How long did it take you to finish your pattern for the first part of the project?
- What part was the hardest for you to wait to do (painting, actually scratching the art)?
- How does this project relate to self-regulation?

CHAPTER 13

Respect Yourself and Others

Respecting ourselves and others covers lots of different behaviors. One thing that respect means is using manners, like saying please and thank you, and being polite to the people around you. It means being honest while being kind.

This is a good opportunity to discuss the Golden Rule: Do unto others as you would have them do unto you. We can show respect other people by treating them in the way we want to be treated. This is especially important when it comes to bullying and teasing. When you recognize that someone else is being bullied, you can make a difference and stand up for them, just as you'd like them to do for you if you were being teased or bullied.

It's also important to recognize that while people may look different, or come from different places, we are all still human, and should be treated equally with respect. You can always find common ground with someone even when they are different from you.

You can also show respect for other people's property. If you're borrowing an item, you treat it with respect and return it when you said you would.

Introductory Discussion Questions

- What does respect mean?

- How can we show respect to ourselves?

- How can you show respect to other kids?

- How can you show respect to adults at school?

- How can you show respect to adults at home?

- How are good manners related to being respectful?

- What does respect have to do with bullying/teasing?

Chrysanthemum and The Wrinkled Heart Activity

This is one of my favorite lessons to do with groups. It's simple, yet visually it makes a big impact. It's a great beginning of the year lesson, to help set the tone for group or classroom interactions.

Materials Needed

- The book *Chrysanthemum* by Kevin Henkes
- One heart cut out of construction paper for every child, plus one for you
- Tape/band-aids

How to Play

- Before you read, pass out the paper hearts to all the group members. Keep one to the side for yourself, and do not use it during the activity.
- Tell the group members to pay attention to whether the characters in the book are using kind words or when characters are using mean words.
- As you read the book, every time a character says something mean to Chrysanthemum, have the kids wrinkle up a piece of their paper heart to represent how mean words impact others.
- Every time Chrysanthemum's parents said something kind and loving to her, have them smooth out the paper heart a little bit and try to repair it.
- At the end of the book try and spread out the heart as much as possible and repair it either using tape or bandages.

Other Ways to Play

Instead of a small heart for everyone, cut out one giant heart. Have kids pass the heart as you read the story.

Debrief Questions

- Compare the paper heart that you set aside at the beginning at all to the ones that were wrinkled during the story. What do you notice about the heart you wrinkled vs. the one that we set aside at the beginning of the story?
- How do mean words impact kids in real life?
- What can you do to make a positive impact on others?

Think Before You Speak Toothpaste Activity

Another simple visual to demonstrate the importance of thinking before you speak, and how even when you apologize, you can't take words back.

Materials Needed

- Tubes of toothpaste
- Paper plates
- Plastic spoon and/or knife

How to Play

Give every group member a tube of toothpaste.

Tell them they need to squeeze all the toothpaste onto their plate.

Once the toothpaste is all out, then give them spoons or knives. Tell them to try to get the toothpaste back into the tube of toothpaste.

Other Ways to Play

Instead of having individual tubes of toothpaste, use one tube for the whole group, and give them each a turn squeezing it out and trying to put it back in.

Debrief Questions

- Which was easier, getting the toothpaste out, or trying to put it back in the tube?
- How does this relate to using respectful words?
- What can you do if you've said something that you regret?

Cotton vs. Sandpaper Words

A great visual and sensory activity to help kids understand which words are more hurtful and which are more gentle.

Materials Needed

- Cotton balls or cotton squares

- Squares of sandpaper

- Two different colors of sticky notes

How to Play

Put out the cotton and the sandpaper and have kids feel them.

As a group, generate words or phrases that people could use with each other in social situations and figure out if they would be considered words that are cotton, or words that are sandpaper. Pick one color sticky note to represent words that are cotton, and one to represent words that are sandpaper.

After discussing as a group, figure out if a word is considered cotton or sandpaper, and write it on the proper sticky note and put it on the wall so everyone can see it.

Other Ways to Play

Use minky fabric, ribbon, or another soft material instead of cotton balls.

Debrief Questions

- Was it easier to come up with cotton words or sandpaper words?

- Were there phrases that were a little more challenging to figure out? What did you do with those words/phrases?

- Do you think you use more cotton words or more sandpaper words?

- How does the tone of someone's voice impact whether the words would be considered cotton or sandpaper?

Compliment Chair

This is a wonderful way for your group to give each other compliments - it's also good practice for kids to learn how to take a compliment. This activity would be good to do as an ending activity, or after you've been working together a while, so the group members have a lot more experiences to pull from to think of compliments.

Materials Needed

- Chair

- Big whiteboard or big poster board

How to Play

Each group member gets a chance to be complimented by the other people in the group. One by one, have each group member sit in the chair, facing away from the white board or the big poster board. While they're sitting and facing forward, the rest of the group writes compliments and kind words all about them. (If you use the poster board, then they can take it home as a keepsake)

Other Ways to Play

Instead of writing things on a board, you can have each group member write their name on a paper bag. Then the bags get passed around the room, and compliments get put into the bag for every person to take home as a keepsake.

Debrief Questions

- How did it feel to give the other group members compliments?

- How did it feel to get compliments?

- Before this, do you remember the last time you were complimented? Or that you complimented someone?

Positive Thoughts Jar

This activity is meant to encourage positive thinking in your group members. Sometimes, kids have a hard time seeing the positives and choose to focus on the negatives. This activity helps them focus on the good things.

Materials Needed

- One jar for every person in the group

- Small squares of paper

How to Play

Talk to the group about the power of positive thinking. You can also introduce the concept of having a growth mindset. You can talk about the power of the word "yet." I don't get it vs. I don't get it yet is a powerful way to shift a child's thinking when they are having difficulty with a concept.

Then tell the group that you're going to practice positive thinking now. Give each person five squares of paper to start, and see what positive things they can think of that they can add to their jar. If they are struggling to figure out positive things to say, give them these prompts:

I can...   I wish..

I am...   I dream...

I hope...

Their jar will be going home with them so that they can add more positive thoughts every day.

Other Ways to Play

Instead of using a jar, give each member a positive thoughts journal. Encourage them to continue to use this journal when they bring it home. Debrief Questions

- How did it go when you were trying to think of positive thoughts?

- How does positive thinking impact you at school? At home?

- What makes it challenging to be positive?

CHAPTER 14

Taking Someone Else's Perspective

Perspective taking is when you can put yourself in someone else's place and imagine how they might see things. It's the ability to view a situation from someone else's point-of-view, or to put yourself in someone else's shoes. This is an important social skill to have.

It's important to understand that just because you feel one way about a certain situation doesn't mean that another person feels that same way. For example, say you and your family get caught in a bad rainstorm. Your dad stays calm, your mom gets worried, and your sister starts to get scared and cries, but you like storms, so you were excited. Even though you all experienced the same rainstorm, you all had different reactions to it. It's important to recognize and acknowledge that your way is not the only way to react to a storm and try to see things from the other family member's perspectives.

Perspective taking matters in friendships too. If you are having a conversation with a friend, you need to be able to think about what they like to talk about and what they enjoy. When you listen and focus on what the other person is interested in, this will more likely lead to a more positive interaction. When you have a good conversation that makes the other person feel happy, you will make a deeper connection with them.

Introductory Discussion Questions

- Do you know what it means to stand in someone else's shoes?

- Why is it important to be able to take another person's perspective?

- Can you share a time when you took someone else's perspective?

- Can you share a time that someone else took your perspective?

Shoes Activity

This activity brings the term "stand in someone else's shoes" to life because this activity involves using other people's shoes to make a smart guess about who they are, and how they might react in certain situations.

Materials Needed

- 5 pairs of different types of shoes (different sizes, shapes, styles, etc.)

- 5 pieces of construction paper or poster board

How to Play

Place the 5 pairs of shoes in front of the 5 pieces of poster board. Explain that as a group, you're going to make smart guesses about the people who belong to these shoes. For each pair of shoes, decide if the person is male or female, how old they are, what grade they're in at school, what they like to do for fun, if they're introverted or extroverted, if they are scared of anything, and any other smart guesses your group wants to make. You can even name the people who belong to the shoes.

Write the information about each "person" on the poster or construction paper in front of their shoe. Once you have a profile for each of the pairs of shoes, then go through the following scenarios, and talk about how each person would react.

How would they feel...

- Going to a birthday party

- Doing a class presentation

- In their dark bedroom at night with a rainstorm outside

- Giving a speech to the whole school

- Going to the doctor

Other Ways to Play

Instead of limiting the people you create to just kids, add in adults too. Add in an older person to represent a parent, or a teacher, or other adult in their lives. Ask the group to think about situations from their perspective.

Debrief Questions

- How was your experience creating the "people" just by using their shoes?

- How did it feel to take their perspectives?

- Can you identify with any of the characters we created?

What Would You Do?

This is an activity that allows children to experience what it would be like if they were unable to use parts of their bodies. This allows them to take the perspective of someone who may have an injury or a disability, and help them consider all the things they are easily able to do that other people are not.

Materials Needed

- Arm slings

- Eye patches or blindfolds

- Crutches

How to Play

Have all group members put on an arm sling, a blindfold, or use the crutches. Have them do the following:

- Tie their shoes

- Write their name

- Put on their backpack

- Walk down the hallway then back

- Add in your own activity, etc.

Have group members switch which item they are wearing (if they were wearing the arm sling, then have them use the crutches). See how that impacts how the ability to accomplish these activities. Do this until all group members have experienced wearing all the different items.

Other Ways to Play

Have half of the group wear the arm sling, blindfold and/or crutches, and then have the other half of the group be their support team, helping them as they try to accomplish those activities. Then switch roles.

Debrief Questions

- Have you ever had a broken arm, or an injured leg, or difficulty seeing before now?

- Which item did you find the most challenging to wear?

- What would have been helpful for you as you were using these items and doing these activities?

Finish the Squiggle

It's so interesting to see how different people see the same simple squiggle.

Materials Needed

- Draw a squiggle on a piece of paper then copy it for each member of the group

- Clipboard/folder/privacy partition

- Arts and crafts supplies

How to Play

Give each member a copy of the squiggle and ask them to complete the picture using the arts and crafts supplies in front of them. Everyone usually sees a different possibility within the same squiggle, so to keep everyone from being influenced by what the others are doing, give them privacy by using clipboards, folders or privacy partitions placed around their work.

Once everyone is done, have each member of the group share what they created.

Other Ways to Play

Read the book *Beautiful Oops* by Barney Saltzberg to give the group some ideas of things they can create with their squiggle.

Debrief Questions

- What did you create?

- How is it different than what other group members created?

- How is it the same as what others created?

Copy the LEGO Creation

The goal of this activity is to make a creation with a set of LEGO bricks and have your partner create the same thing. You have to communicate with each other to make this happen, WITHOUT looking at the actual LEGO bricks. Think about how the other person will see the structure and talk them through making it.

Materials Needed

- Sets of LEGO bricks - 2 identical set of bricks for each pair of group members
- Privacy divider/folder

How to Play

Divide the group into pairs.

- Each person in the pair gets one set of the LEGO bricks.

- Decide who will make a design first and have them create it.

- The person who made the creation communicates with their partner about how the creation should look. They could draw about it, write out the steps or say the steps out loud to their partner. Think about how the other person sees the LEGO bricks. Be descriptive. How do you accurately describe how to arrange the pieces?

- Your partner tries to make the same LEGO bricks creation.

- Next, you switch roles. Your partner now takes a turn creating a design and explaining it to you.

It's okay if you don't get it right, this is a challenging activity!

Other Ways to Play

- Start with just a few LEGO bricks to begin with, then add more to make it harder.
- Or instead of using LEGOs, use K'NEX, wooden blocks or some other building material.

Debrief Questions

- What was the most challenging part of this activity?

- Which did you prefer - making the creation and telling how to make it, or being told how to make the creation?

- How did you and your partner work together?

This is a creative way to practice figuring out what different people might say or do, or what they may be thinking or feeling.

Make Your Own Comic Strip

Materials Needed

- Comic Strip (pgs 167-168)

- Pencils

How to Play

Give every person in the group their own comic strip. Have kids fill in the thought and talk bubbles. Once everyone is done, have them share what they wrote.

Other Ways to Play

- Instead of doing the comic strip individually, have kids break into pairs or create the comic strip as a group.

- Use a blank comic strip and have kids illustrate the scenes themselves.

- Cut out pictures from magazines. Put thought bubbles and talk bubbles by each person, and come up with ideas for what they are thinking and saying.

Debrief Questions

- What was your comic strip about?

- How is it different than what other group members created?

- How is it the same as what others created?

- How was your experience coming up with a storyline and dialogue for your comic strip?

165

Picking Up on Clues

Being a child with good social skills means being able to pay attention to what's going on around you and react in an expected way. Kids need to be able to pick up on clues from others in different social scenarios. For instance, they need to be able to pick up on the social rules for playgrounds and at recess. They need to understand that they shouldn't walk through a basketball game or cut the line in a foursquare game. For example, what are the social rules for swings? Where do you wait for your turn to go on the swings?

It's also helpful for kids to be able to pick up on clues in school. If all the kids in a class are quietly sitting working in their math book, your child would benefit from picking up on those clues, taking out their math book, looking at the board for page numbers and start working. They also need to pick up on facial expressions, emotions, and intentions of others. Being able to pick up on these clues will help them figure out what they should be doing in social situations.

There's also something known as the "hidden" social curriculum. There are social rules that are explicitly stated in places, like "No running in the halls" or "Use Respectful language." But then there are those rules which aren't explicitly stated, like that the elevator is off limits or how kids clean up after lunch and go out to recess (they first clear the tables, then stack the chairs, then are called by table to line up and go outside). It's an important social skill that kids not only learn and understand the explicit rules but also those rules that are part of the "hidden" curriculum.

Introductory Discussion Questions

- How does picking up on clues help you in friendships?
- How does picking up on clues help you at school?
- How does picking up on clues help you at home?
- What are some hidden rules at school?
- What are some hidden rules in your house?

Decode the Message

This is a fun way for kids to practice uncovering the clues and make smart guesses about who created the sentence they translated.

Materials Needed

- Secret Code handout (pg 171)

- Strips of paper

- Pencils

- Basket

How to Play

Have kids take the secret code and come up with a simple sentence to translate. Have kids write their sentence in code. Then put all of their codes in the basket. Have each child pick out a code (make sure it's not the one they created!) and have them translate the code. Then have them guess which group member wrote the code.

Other Ways to Play

- Use two or three different secret codes – maybe one with numbers and one with shapes. Make sure kids are using the right one to decode their secret message.

- Have kids make up their own codes using shapes, numbers, letters or some combination.

Debrief Questions

- What was your experience like creating the code?

- How did it go when you were translating someone else's code?

- Which did you prefer?

- How did you figure out who wrote the sentence you translated?

SECRET CODE

A = D	N = Q
B = E	O = R
C = F	P = S
D = G	Q = T
E = H	R = U
F = I	S = V
G = J	T = W
H = K	U = X
I = L	V = Y
J = M	W = Z
K = N	X = A
L = O	Y = B
M = P	Z = C

Secret Positive Messages

This is another creative way to write a secret message and have kids reveal it. Plus it's relaxing to paint using watercolors.

Materials Needed

- White crayons
- White paper
- Watercolors

How to Play

The kids can use the white crayons on the white paper to write secret messages to each other. To reveal the messages, have them use the watercolor paints, and paint over the white paper where the message is written. The message should appear once the paint is applied to the paper. They can do it over and over again for tons of fun!

Other Ways to Play

- Have kids write compliments to another group member and give it to them to reveal.
- Use lemon juice to write messages and heat it over a light bulb to reveal the message.

Debrief Questions

- How did you come up with your secret message?
- Are there any messages you wish you could give to a friend?
- Are there messages you wish you could give to a family member?

What's Missing?

This activity requires kids to use their powers of observation and memory to pay attention to the items.

Materials Needed

- 15 random items

- Tray

How to Play

Start the group with the tray and 15 items visible. Go through each item and have kids hold them, so they know what it is and agree on what it is called.

Explain that you'll be removing one item from the tray and kids have to guess which item it is.

Go into another space where kids can't see you for a moment and remove an item. Then come back in the room and have kids guess which item is missing.

Then have group members take turns coming out into the hall with you and removing the items.

Finally, start to move the items around on the tray to make this activity more challenging.

Other Ways to Play

- Have kids bring in materials to use for the activity.

- Make it easier - reduce the number of items on the tray.

- Make it harder - increase the number of items on the tray.

Debrief Questions

- Why do you think we went through each of the items at the beginning of group?

- How was it trying to figure out which item was missing?

- What was your experience picking out an item to take away?

- How did the challenge change when we started moving items around on the tray?

DIY I Spy

This is an opportunity for kids to practice their creativity by making their very own I Spy book.

Materials Needed

- Several sets of stickers
- Paper
- Pencils/colored pencils/crayons/markers
- I Spy Books (as examples)

How to Play

Explain that kids will be making their own I Spy books. If they've never seen one, have them look at one, so they can see an example. Fold a piece of paper in half. Have kids take stickers and make a sticker scene on one half of the page. Then have them write down 3 or 4 things to find on the other side. Have them complete three pages, then staple them together for their own DIY I Spy book.

Once they're done, have kids look through each other's I Spy books.

Other Ways to Play

- Instead of using stickers, use real toys and set up scenes. Take pictures and print them out.
- Make an I Spy jar using rice and small figures. Make a list of the items in the bottle to find, and tape it to the front of the bottle. Superglue the lid of the bottle shut.

Debrief Questions

- How did you come up with your ideas for your I Spy pages?
- How was it writing the clues for the I Spy pages?
- How was it reading and finding clues that another one of your group members made?

One Change

This activity helps kids pay attention to specifics about another person's appearance.

Materials Needed

- Dress up items, like fake mustache, hats, eyepatch, scarves

How to Play

Explain to the group that they are going to be detectives and they're going to have to use their powers of observation to solve a mystery. They have to think with their eyes.

To start, stand in front of the group and have them study your appearance: what you're wearing, your hair, your jewelry, etc. Then go out into the hall and change one thing. Choose something easy first, like putting on a hat or a fake mustache. When you come back in, tell them to raise their hand when they see what looks different.

Then go out again and switch something a little more challenging, like moving rings to another finger or putting your shoes on the wrong feet. Once they figure it out, then it's time for the group to have some fun. Have each person in the group take turns going out and switching one thing about themselves and seeing if the group can guess the change.

Other Ways to Play

- Include other adults or kids from outside the group in this activity.

- Use American Girl® Dolls or paper dolls.

Debrief Questions

- Which change was the easiest for you to pick out?

- Which change was the hardest?

- How was it looking for changes?

- How did it go deciding what you wanted to change?

Favorite Group Games

Games are one of the best ways to work on social skills. Playing a game requires patience, being able to wait and take turns, cooperating with others, negotiating about who goes first, agreeing to and sticking to the rules, and being a good sport, whether you win or lose. You can practice so many social skills simply by playing a game. Here are 10 of my favorite games to play in a group.

Apples to Apples Junior®

I love this game because players have to think about someone else's perspective. What card will be chosen as the winner will change depending on who is judging, so players need to adjust how they play and what they pick based on which person making the final decision.

Hedbanz®

You pick a card, put it in your headband, and then ask the other people playing with you yes or no questions to try and figure out what you are. You have to think of the kinds of questions you need to ask to get you closer to your answer. This is a wonderful game to work on perspective taking, being a flexible thinker, and communicating. Plus it can be hilarious!

Would You Rather?®

This is a fun game that helps kids practice decision making. You can also make it more creative and fun by making up your own would you rather questions to ask each other during the group.

Q's Race to the Top®

This game is one of my new favorite social skills games! The game has three types of cards: Blue YOU Cards with questions to answer about yourself or your feelings, Green Q Cards with questions related to social skills and Orange DO Cards, which have movement activities. The counselor in me loves the Blue and Green cards, and the mom in me loves the Orange cards. They get kids moving and doing physical things that are fun and a little challenging. Having the physical component is the perfect way to balance out the talking parts of the game.

Rory's Story Cubes®

This game encourages creativity, flexible thinking and working together to create a story using nine cubes with different images. This game is excellent for small groups!

Bubble Talk®

This game is similar to Apples to Apples but uses pictures and captions instead. Everyone takes a turn being the judge, and the judge picks the caption that they think fits the image best. You have to think about things from the perspective of the judge, so it's another game to help children work on taking another person's perspective.

UNO

This game is very popular, but it can be tricky because different people play by different rules. It's important to make sure to talk with group members before the game begins so everyone is on the same page when someone picks up a draw 4 or changes the color.

Connect 4

Another game that I love playing in groups with kids. Sometimes kids would play tournaments, or have conversations about whether they played offensively (focused on winning) versus defensively (focused on preventing the other person from winning). It's simple to set up and can be played in so many different ways.

Jenga®

Jenga is one of my favorite games to play with a small group. The game Jenga in and of itself is fun, but I love writing my own questions on the Jenga blocks to enhance the interactions. You can get multiple Jenga games and write different types of questions on each set. You could write one as a getting to know you Jenga, another as coping skills Jenga, etc.

There is also a therapeutic game called **Totika®** which has four different sets of questions you can use with colored blocks that you stack just like Jenga - answering questions that correspond to colors. Whether you create your own or use Totika, it's a great way to spark conversations in group.

Peaceable Kingdom Games

These games are designed to make sure that there is no "winner" or "loser," but all the players work together toward a common goal. Some of my favorites are:

- Hoot Owl Hoot®

- Race to The Treasure®

- Dinosaur Escape®

- Cauldron Quest®

- Mole Rats in Space®

- Listmania®

Great Group Activities

Create Story Stones

Gather smooth stones and permanent markers to create your own story stones. Have group members draw different images on the stones, and then combine them to create a story (as you would with Story Cubes®).

Another way to make story stones would be to use images that are already printed. Cut them out and use Mod Podge® to attach them to the stones. Have fun making a DIY game as a group that you can use over and over again.

Make a Game Together

Work together to create your own game. It could be a board game, a card game, or another type. Talk as a group about what you'd like to create, come up with the rules of the game, and figure out what you need to play (board game, pieces, start/finish lines, etc.). Divide the tasks up among the group members, and work together to make the game come to life. Once it's all done, play the game you created. And you can invite other people to play your game too!

Create a Story with Illustrations Together

Maybe you have an especially artistic group, and you want to make something together. Try creating and illustrating an entire story. Work on the plot, and write the story together as a group. Then have group members illustrate different parts of the story. Once it's all done, share your story with others.

Design Your Perfect School

Discuss as a group the perfect school. Talk about how the days would be structured, what kind of classes would be available, and how the building itself would look. Then work together to draw what you discussed or create a 3D structure representing all the things you discussed.

Make a Stop-Motion Video

Stop motion is such a cool medium, but this will require a lot of patience and attention to detail. By taking pictures of a scene, then connecting them all, you get a cool video. Think about which items would work well for stop-motion - clay, Stikbots®, small bendable figures, etc. Create a short storyline for your stop motion video. Then use a camera or smartphone to take pictures of scenes, then move the figures slightly, and take another picture. Keep going until you have several pictures to connect in a video.

If you're new to stop-motion, then try using a stop motion animation/claymation kit, or app to create videos. These things are designed to help make it easier for you to create your stop motion videos. Some apps show you the picture you just took overlaid with the current image you are going to shoot. They also allow you to play it back, and add sounds, music, and special effects. It's a simple way to get started.

Create a Play

Creating a whole play could be a project that could be completed over several weeks as a group. Create a storyline, come up with characters and write their dialogue, create sets and practice. Finally, invite people to come and see you put on your play.

Project Beautify

There are always areas to improve in schools or local neighborhoods. It doesn't have to be a huge project. Even something simple can have a huge impact. Pick a spot that you want to beautify. It could be a blank wall, and you want to create a mural, or an empty plot that you want to turn into a small garden, or something else! Use your problem-solving skills to work together as a group to generate ideas for a spot to beautify, pick your spot, then make a plan for how you are going to improve the spot (of course, get permission first!) What an awesome project for a group to do together!

I hope you have discovered some great ideas for building social skills through play. I'd love to hear from you about how activities went with your group or other activities you were inspired to create to help kids learn these critical life skills. Feel free to email me at janine@encourageplay.com or share to our Facebook page!

Want more ideas? Visit encourageplay.com today!

Books to Read

Listening

Howard B. Wigglebottom Learns to Listen by Howard Binkow

Whole Body Listening Larry at Home by Elizabeth Sautter and Kristen Wilson

Whole Body Listening Larry at School by Elizabeth Sautter and Kristen Wilson

Problem Solving

What Do You Do With a Problem? by Kobi Yamada and Mae Besom

Beautiful Oops by Barney Saltzberg

Ada Twist, Scientist by Andrea Beaty

Rafa and the Mist by Kade Baird

Flexibility

Not a box by Antoinette Portis

Not a stick by Antoinette Portis

Duck! Rabbit! by Amy Krouse Rosenthal and Tom Lichtenheld

My day is ruined! by Bryan Smith

Your Fantastic Elastic Brain by JoAnn Deak, Ph.D.

The Girl Who Never Made Mistakes by Mark Pett and Gary Rubinstein

Mistakes that Worked: 40 Familiar Inventions & How They Came to Be by Charlotte Foltz Jones and John O'Brien

Working Together

The Gigantic Turnip by Aleksei Tolstoy

Teamwork Isn't My Thing, and I Don't Like to Share! (Best Me I Can Be!) by Julia Cook

Swimmy by Leo Lionni

Taking Turns

Share and Take Turns by Cheri J. Miners

Waiting Is Not Easy by Mo Willems

That's Not Mine by Anna Kang

How to Share with a Bear by Eric Pinder

Teamwork Isn't My Thing, and I Don't Like to Share by Julia Cook

Personal Space

Personal Space Camp by Julia Cook

Miles is the Boss of His Body by Samantha Kurtzman-Counter and Abbie Schiller

I Said No! A Kid-to-kid Guide to Keeping Private Parts Private by Kimberly and Zack King

Being Kind

Each Kindness by Jacqueline Woodson and E. B. Lewis

Kindness is Cooler Mrs. Ruler by Margery Cuyler

Ordinary Mary's Extraordinary Deed by Emily Pearson

We're all Wonders by R.J. Palacio

One by Kathryn Otoshi

Enemy Pie by Derek Munson

What Does It Mean to be Kind? by Rana DiOrio and Stephane Jorisch

Feelings Identification

How Are You Peeling? by Saxton Freymann and Joost Elffers

The Way I Feel by Janan Cain

Today I Feel Silly: And Other Moods That Make My Day by Jamie Lee Curtis

Happiness doesn't come from Headstands by Tamara Leavitt

Each of these authors has a series of books about different feelings

Julia Cook (covers topics like worry, anger, and bad attitudes, grief,etc.)

Dawn Heubner (covers worry/anxiety, jealousy, negativity, anger, shyness, etc.)

Trevor Romain (stress, grief, anger, etc.)

Andi Green (worry, loneliness, frustration, etc.)

Coping with Feelings

Yoga and Mindfulness Practices for Children Activity and Coloring Book by Jennifer Cohen Harper

Wilma Jean the Worry Machine Activity and Idea Book by Julia Cook

The Secret to Clara's Calm by Tamara Leavitt

Coping Skills for Kids Workbook by Janine Halloran (that's me!)

Self-Regulation

Listening to My Body by Gabi Garcia

The Most Magnificent Thing by Ashley Spires

Master of Mindfulness: How to Be Your Own Superhero in Times of Stress by Laurie Grossman and Mr. Musumeci's 5th Grade Class

Puppy Mind by Andrew Jordan Nance and Jim Durk

The Lemonade Hurricane: A Story of Mindfulness and Meditation by Licia Morelli and Jennifer E. Morris

A Handful of Quiet: Happiness in Four Pebbles by Thich Nhat Hanh

Respect for Yourself

Have You Filled a Bucket Today? by Carol McCloud

Berenstain Bears and Too Much Teasing by Stan Berenstain and Jan Berenstain

Wonder by R.J. Palacio

The Hundred Dresses by Eleanor Estes

Taking someone else's perspective

Spoon by Amy Krouse Rosenthal

Stand in My Shoes by Bob Sornson

How Do I Stand in Your Shoes? by Susan DeBell

Optical Illusions by DK Publishing

Paying Attention

I Spy Treasure Hunt by Jean Marzollo

Where's Waldo? Deluxe Edition by Martin Handford

Once Upon a Time: Picture Puzzles to Search and Solve by Walter Wick

Search and Find National Parks by Maud Lienard

Can You Find It?: Search and Discover More Than 150 Details in 19 Works of Art by Judith Cressy

Practice Picking Up On Clues

Books that have unexpected things happen are always fun. Here are some ideas, however, you can also speak with your school librarian. Read a small passage from the book. Then stop and have kids guess what happened next.

Mo Willems books

The Chocolate Touch

Sideways Stories from Wayside School

Bad Kitty

The 13 Story Treehouse

Diary of a Wimpy Kid

The Percy Jackson Series

Other Resources/Ideas

Flexibility

Rigid Thinking® - Resource from Autism Teaching Strategies

A Flexible Thinking Story: The Invention of Chewing Gum - available on Teachers Pay Teachers

Mixed Up Day - Do things in a different order during group, and see how it goes!

Communication

I highly recommend pre-screening movies or tv shows before you show it during a group. If you're watching a show and you notice a scene that would be great, make a note of it and show it when you get a chance! Some of my best inspiration for tv shows or movies to use has happened when I'm watching tv or movies with my own kids.

- Ideas for things you can point out in tv or movie clips

    - Body language

    - When a character's body language doesn't match what they say

    - When the emphasis on a particular word changes the meaning of a sentence

    - When the tone of voice has an impact on the meaning of a sentence

Personal Space

Watch a video clip of the Close Talker from Seinfeld® to discuss personal space.

Being Kind

Great Kindness Challenge - thegreatkindnesschallenge.com

Kindness Elves - thekindnesselves.com

Boom Boom Cards - boomboomcards.com

Little Loving Hands - a subscription box where you can create items to donate!

Coping with Feelings

Stress Free Kids - stressfreekids.com

Go Zen - gozen.com

GoNoodle - gonoodle.com

Coping Skills for Kids - copingskillsforkids.com

Respect for Yourself

Kid President - How to Disagree

Amazing Kids of Character: Respect

Sesame Street Video about Respect

Bibliography

For your convenience, purchasers can download
and print handouts from pesi.com/socialskills

About CASEL. (2018). Retrieved from https://casel.org/about-2/

Brown, S. L., & Vaughan, C. C. (2010). *Play: how it shapes the brain, opens the imagination, and invigorates the soul.* New York: Avery.

Core SEL Competencies. (2017). Retrieved from https://casel.org/core-competencies/

Fiorelli, J. A. & Russ, S. W. (2012) Pretend Play, Coping, and Subjective Well-Being in Children: A Follow-Up Study. *American Journal of Play*, 5(1), 81-103.

Ginsburg, K. R., Jablow, M. M., & Ginsburg, K. R. (2011). Building resilience in children and teens: Giving kids roots and wings. Elk Grove Village, IL: American Academy of Pediatrics.

Gray, Peter (2013) *Free to Learn: Why Unleashing the Instinct to Play Will Make Our Children Happier, More Self-Reliant, and Better Students for Life.* New York: Basic Books.

Hughes, B. (2002) *A Playworker's Taxonomy of Play Types.* 2nd Edition, Play Education.

Hurley, K. (2015). The happy kid handbook: how to raise joyful children in a stressful world. New York: Tarcher.

J., Layard, R., & Sachs, J. (2015, April 2). *World Happiness Report.* [Government Report] Retrieved from http://worldhappiness.report/wp-content/uploads/sites/2/2015/04/ WHR15_Sep15. pdf Report of *Healthy Development: A Summit on Young Children's Mental Health.* Partnering with Communication Scientists, Collaborating across Disciplines and Leveraging Impact to Promote Children's Mental Health. 2009. Washington, DC: Society for Research in Child Development

Lavoie, R.D., Levine, M.D., Reiner, R., & Reiner, M. (2006). *It's so much work to be your friend: helping the child with learning disabilities find social success.* New York: Simon & Schuster.

Parten, M (1932). "Social participation among preschool children". *Journal of Abnormal and Social Psychology* 28 (3): 136–147.

Made in the USA
Columbia, SC
30 January 2020